'...a nice summary of the Bible's humoune
humour, which includes irony, sarcasm,
35 categories) Each discussion also inc
(and others) today. In brief, humour is l
ourselves. There is a real place for hum
need to be careful how we use it. The au
through each of the books of the Bible, giving examples.'
- Robert C. Newman, Emeritus Professor of New Testament and Christian Evidences, Missio Seminary, Philadelphia, Pennsylvania, and Emeritus Director of the Interdisciplinary Biblical Research Institute, M.Div. (FTS), STM in OT (BTS), see https://www.amazon.com/Robert-C.-Newman/e/B071181B6S

'… an unusual and thought-provoking book about humour in the Bible. He helpfully highlights the ways in which humour appears in the Bible to give us a better understanding of the Lord and of ourselves. The systematic approach of working through the books of the Bible gives new insights into all sorts of passages.'
- Joe Dent, Minister of St Andrew's Church, Plymouth, UK.

'David Legg has had a refined and sensitive sense of humour for many a year; and now he applies it to the pages of Scripture in a way that few other authors have, to fascinating and stimulating effect. You don't have to agree with every judgement he makes here to be benefitted by it in your understanding of God's holy word. And in case you are wondering about the whole topic, I was reminded of what I read in C R Vaughan's 19th century Banner of Truth classic, The Gifts of the Holy Spirit, many years ago: that regeneration affects the sense of wit and humour, and that these are so much part of our created nature that they are likely to exist in heaven as well. I commend this study warmly.'
- Chris Bennett leads Wilton Community Church and lectures at the London Seminary (UK), on Preaching, New Testament, Old Testament and Hebrew.

David Legg ministered in Devon (UK), and now lives and writes in Hampshire. Other publications include *The Genesis Roller-coaster*, *Covenants for Evangelicals*, and *The Songs of Ascents and Eight Last Davidic Psalms (26 Discussion Bible Studies in Psalms 120 to 145)*. He is married to Sue; they have three sons, and a daughter-in-law.

Humour in the Holy Bible? Can you really be serious? Yes; in fact, when the Bible is humorous, it is often at its most serious. This book defines biblical humour, explains the humour in all the 66 books except a handful. It even looks briefly at the Apocrypha, in order to see how their non-biblical humour is different from that of scripture.

Importantly, this book then applies what we learn from humorous passages in the Bible. If we fail to notice and understand the intentionally humorous passages in scripture, we will also misapply them. Biblical humour is rarely 'funny-ha-ha', but it is always important. Biblical humour helps us to enjoy our God. It protects us from sinful pride, because laughing at ourselves helps us to be humble. Biblical humour strengthens and builds our faith in a powerful way. We should never laugh at God, but we should always laugh with him! Find out how, in this unique book.

For Rob, Helen, Rachel, Toby and Nathan, with thanks.

Humour in the Bible?

You canNOT be SERIOUS!

David W. Legg

COVENANT BOOKS UK

10 Kelsey Close, Liss. GU33 7HR

Email: dwlegg@gmail.com

Website: http://davidlegg.org.uk/

© David W. Legg 2019

David W. Legg has asserted his right under the Copyright, Designs and Patents Act, 1988, UK, to be identified as the author of this work.

All rights reserved. No part of this publication may be reproduced, stored in a retrieval system or transmitted in any form or by any means, electronic, mechanical, photocopying, recording or otherwise, without prior permission of the author or other copyright holders.

Bible quotations:

NIV2011: THE HOLY BIBLE, NEW INTERNATIONAL VERSION®, NIV® Copyright © 1973, 1978, 1984, 2011 by Biblica, Inc.® Used by permission.
All rights reserved worldwide.

ESV: Scripture quotations are from the ESV® Bible (The Holy Bible, English Standard Version®), copyright © 2001 by Crossway, a publishing ministry of Good News Publishers. Used by permission. All rights reserved. May not copy or download more than 500 consecutive verses of the ESV Bible or more than one half of any book of the ESV Bible.

NET Bible: Scripture quoted by permission. Quotations designated (NET) are from the NET Bible® copyright ©1996-2016 by Biblical Studies Press, L.L.C. http://netbible.com All rights reserved.

KJV/AV: public domain.

Photographs and diagrams are all owned by the author, except where indicated.

Artwork © Rose Bell https://www.rose-bell.com/

Created in LibreOffice 6 with open source software running on Fedora 29 Linux.

First published 2019. ISBN: 9781081284763

Contents

1. Introduction............................7
2. Humour in the Pentateuch........18
   2.1 Genesis............................18
   2.3 Exodus............................23
   2.3 Leviticus.........................26
   2.4 Numbers..........................26
   2.5 Deuteronomy.....................29
3. Humour in the History Books...30
   3.1 Joshua............................30
   3.2 Judges............................32
   3.3 Ruth...............................35
   3.4 I and II Samuel..................36
   3.5 I and II Kings....................40
   3.6 I and II Chronicles.............42
   3.7 Ezra...............................45
   3.8 Nehemiah.........................46
   3.9 Esther.............................46
4. Humour In The Wisdom Books49
   4.1 Job................................49
   4.2 Psalms............................51
   4.3 Proverbs..........................54
   4.4 Ecclesiastes......................57
   4.5 The Song of Songs (or of
   Solomon)..............................61
5. Humour in the Major Prophets. 62
   5.1 Isaiah.............................62
   5.2 Jeremiah..........................64
   5.3 Lamentations.....................65
   5.4 Ezekiel............................66
   5.5 Daniel.............................68
6. Humour in the Minor Prophets. 72
   6.1 Hosea.............................72
   6.2 Joel...............................73
   6.3 Amos..............................73
   6.4 Obadiah...........................75
6.5 Jonah...............................75
6.6 Micah..............................78
6.7 Nahum.............................79
6.8 Habakkuk.........................79
6.9 Zephaniah.........................81
6.10 Haggai............................82
6.11 Zechariah........................83
6.12 Malachi...........................85
7. Humour in the Apocrypha?.......87
8. Humour in the Gospels............89
   8.1 Matthew..........................89
   8.2 Mark..............................102
   8.3 Luke..............................105
   8.4 John..............................111
8. Humour in Acts....................113
9. Humour in Paul's Letters.......118
   9.1 Romans...........................118
   9.2 I Corinthians.....................119
   9.3 II Corinthians....................121
   9.4 Galatians.........................122
   9.5 Ephesians........................123
   9.6 Philippians.......................123
   9.7 Colossians.......................124
   9.8 I and II Thessalonians.......124
   9.9 I and II Timothy...............125
   9.10 Titus............................125
   9.11 Philemon........................126
10. Humour in the Other Letters.127
   10.1 Hebrews.........................127
   10.2 James............................128
   10.3 I and II Peter...................130
   10.4 I, II and III John.............132
   10.5 Jude.............................132
   10.6 Revelation.......................132
11. Conclusion..........................134

****

1. Introduction

A father was reading from the sermon on the mount[1] to his four-year-old, when the boy burst out laughing. He laughed because he immediately saw how ridiculous it would be for a small organ such as the human eye to contain a *'beam'*[2] as narrated in Matthew 7:3. The child had seen a funny side to what Jesus said. The adults were soberly contemplating Jesus' severe warning against hypocrisy. Although the overall lesson may not yet have been appreciated by the four-year-old, he had noticed something in the passage, something in Jesus' teaching style, that the adults had missed: Humour.

The adult attitude to the discovery of humour in scripture is likely to be, "What? You cannot be serious!" And so said the tennis player John McEnroe in 1981 when his 'ace' was ruled 'out' by the Wimbledon umpire. *"You can't be serious"*, he said. And as his temper flared, *"You canNOT be SERIOUS!"* He may have been right that *"that ball was on the line!"*, but he was wrong to doubt the umpire's *seriousness*.

In much of life there is conflict between seriousness and humour to the extent that we struggle to be both serious and humorous at the same time. It is hard to be both funny and sober. We usually reserve humour for those occasions, contexts and those social situations, where there is nothing sombre or weighty going on. So, when we bump into humour in the Bible, we skip over it, and immediately try to discern the eternal, serious, truth being taught. Often, we completely fail to recognise that the writer, the speaker, or the Teacher, was employing humour, unless we are four years old and hearing it read for the very first time.

---
1   Matthew 5 to 7
2   A *plank* or *log* nowadays

On hearing the possibility that scripture might indeed contain humour, I too was suspicious; the hackles rose, the antenna was up; I was listening for heresy. But the antenna was also up and listening for possible examples of humour in the Bible, during Bible readings, during sermons, during the study of scripture.

So, when a visiting preacher came to preach at a summer Sunday evening service, I was subconsciously prepared for what transpired. Now the evening service in England was well and truly in decline by this time, so all the attenders were serious, even erudite, thoughtful, and deeply respectful of scripture. Why else would they turn out on a Sunday evening when they could have been chilling in front of the 'one-eyed god in the corner' of their living rooms, or having a barbecue with friends? On that evening, songs and hymns and spiritual songs were sung, all of them serious, all of them leading towards the pinnacle of the evening's worship experience.

Eventually the scripture passage was read, 1 Samuel 5. It was read well, too. The gripping story of how the ark of the covenant, *the* most holy object that God's people had, was stolen by the uncircumcised Philistines, had everyone paying full attention in order to hear how the shocking events unfolded. There was complete concentration and stony silence. There was tacit consternation about how such a sacrilegious event could ever have taken place. How could this have been recorded in holy scripture? The stony silence ruled, except in the front row, where some clearly unspiritual dolt was laughing his socks off.

Now it has to be conceded that there is not much that is funny in early 1 Samuel. Chapter 4 ends with a fatality, as *Ichabod* is born, and his mother dies with the words, *"The glory has departed"*, on her lips. The very *ark of the LORD* itself *had been captured* by the Philistine enemy. Actually, chapter 5 is just as serious, and even more people die; but something happens in the narrative that not everyone in the congregation at first appreciated. The preacher stood up to introduce the passage. The change in the narrative was so important, he said, that he had previously intended, whilst in his study preparing, to rebuke the congregation for not listening properly to the Bible reading. But, due to the dolt in the front row, he was now unable to administer a thorough rebuke to everyone. At least one person had been enjoying the passage, hearing the humour, and, laughing his socks off!

What was there to laugh at in a chapter with such a high body count? Well, the false god, *Dagon*, gets single-handedly defeated by the *ark of the LORD*. First, he is made to bow down in front of the true God, as represented by the presence of the *ark*. Next, the Philistines stand him up again. That a god should need to be stood up is funny. The next morning, Dagon is in an even worse state, not only bowing down before the *ark*, but also with his hands broken off! You could almost feel sorry for this godlet. Not only so, but his head had broken off and was lying together with his severed hands on the threshold of the dagonic temple. What are the priests of Dagon to do now that their god is not only humiliated but also mutilated? Well, they consecrate the place where he fell by being very careful not to tread just there—an act of true love and devotion to their fallen god. Presumably they then stood him up again[3]!

Now anyone noticing the verbal clues in the above summary of the story will be tempted to find it just a little bit funny. When narrating humour in Western English culture we include little clues to lift the mood and give the reader a sign that the narrative is intended to be amusing: '*godlet*', '*dagonic*' etc. But when read well, even in translation from Hebrew to English, anyone who is truly loyal to the LORD, who enjoys this account, simply has to admit that it is pricelessly funny.

The humour continues all the way through to the very end of 1 Samuel 6 where, suddenly, the people of *Beth Shemesh* casually look inside the *ark of the LORD* and are *struck down*, all *seventy* of them[4]. What is going on in these uncomfortable chapters? Do they demonstrate that it is quite possible for humour and sobriety to co-exist in scripture? Certainly, but more than that: They show how an important and true story is made even more striking, memorable and enjoyable, even more serious, by the sudden jolts from serious to humorous and then back again to downright morbid. In fact, we can safely say that when the Bible is at its funniest, it is also at its most serious. So we had better take note very carefully when we detect that a biblical writer is deploying the weapon of humour!

Back in the sermon on the mount, there is not an incongruous contradiction of mood here. When Jesus taught us about having a *plank* in our eyes to warn us about hypocrisy, he combined humour and severity in a thoroughly compatible way. He thereby helps us to learn the lesson, remember it, and act on it daily.

Humour in the Bible? It could not be more serious.

****

---

3   In his commentary on 1 Samuel, Dale Ralph Davis points out that there are various puns in the original Hebrew text, which serve to confirm how funny the incident is, but without detracting from its seriousness.

4   Some ancient manuscripts actually say 50,070 died, but that may be more than the local population.

And yet, there is a little part of us that is still scared to admit to the co-existence of material in the word of God that is both humorous and holy. We are right to be wary. John Frame writes that although...

'... humor(sic) *that demeans God or his image in us is wrong, good humor is a wonderful remedy to pride and despair'*.[5]

Humour in the Bible laughs at us, never at God. So humour tends to be in the narrative passages, where stories are happening, and people are doing things, saying things, making mistakes, learning, repenting, humbling themselves, failing, laughing, doubting and trusting.

Some biblical books seem devoid of humour, for example Leviticus. Perhaps it would be inappropriate for a book devoted to the subject of the holiness of God to employ humour? However, in the book of Genesis, there is not only plenty of divine activity, but there are also plenty of human goings-on too. Genesis has God, in his sovereignty, blessing his creation. Mankind, in their sin, ruin it. Since most of Genesis is narrative, i.e. stories, there is plenty of scope for humour, and even a superficial study of Genesis will reveal that the author had a sense of humour.

The major prophets have some humour, the minor prophets very little, except Jonah. His book is a single, integrated, exercise in humour. But the humour is all aimed at humans, not at God.

The synoptic gospels, Matthew, Mark and Luke, are packed with Jesus' own humour, but John has very little. In general the narrative books have plenty of humour, but the purely didactic[6] have very little. Luke never misses an opportunity in his gospel and in Acts, but Paul rarely lightens up, just occasionally allowing himself a bit of rather gothic humour.

God gives grace (to put it theologically) and shows favour (to put it relationally) to the humble[7]. Who are these humble people who receive much-needed grace and favour from their God? They are God's people, who take his word seriously. If we take it seriously in the way that God intended, we must also notice where scripture is being humorous. Given that the butt of the humour is usually the humans in the biblical story, it must be the case that the humble are, in fact, those who can laugh at themselves. If we are proud, we will find it difficult to laugh at ourselves. If humble, we might even enjoy the joke at our own expense, humble ourselves, repent, and then continue receiving the promised grace and favour from our God.

---

5   The Doctrine of the Christian Life, p507, John Frame, P&R, 2008.

6   teaching

7   Proverbs 3:34

Humour deals with our pride. Humour makes it easier for us to accept bad news. Humour thereby helps us to accept the good news. By showing us how foolish we can be, humour helps to become wise.

Furthermore, correctly identifying humour in scripture helps us to interpret passages as the writer intended. Often, biblical humour makes us smile, and is obviously intended to help us to be patient in difficult circumstances. It lifts the mood, strengthens our resolve to follow Jesus, and releases a few pheromones to help us enjoy[8] God's grace, forgiveness, patience and promised blessings.

Francis Schaeffer wrote that, *'while Christians do many things to serve the Lord, it is obvious from our faces and our conversations that few enjoy him.'* [9]

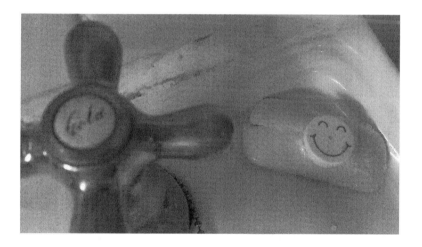

At home, we have a smiley magnetic soap holder. Apparently we humans are programmed to smile back at people who smile at us. It is claimed that this even works with printed smiles on soap magnets[10]. The smile reflex is involuntary, so despite our best efforts at self-control, we smile anyway and release some biochemicals into our bloodstreams, and feel better, happier, and more robust. In other words, laughing at the destruction of a *Dagon* not only strengthens our faith in the true *God*, but also makes us feel better. We share smiles with those around us, who, in turn, also feel better. Everyone

---

8   Westminster Shorter Catechism 1646/7 '*Q.1: What is the chief end of man? A. Man's chief end is to glorify God, and to enjoy him forever.*' We can easily forget that last part.
9   *The Sunday School Times*, June 16th and 23rd, 1951, quoted in '*Francis Schaeffer, an Authentic Life*', 2008, p103, IVP
10 This also confirms that it is a retrograde step to dispense with soap in favour of squirty antibacterial detergent.

enjoys the defeat of *Dagon*. This kind of interaction is important, a part of real fellowship; it glorifies *God* in a way that is consistent with how he created us; our feelings agree with our reason. Everybody wins, except *Dagon* and the *Philistines*, of course.

****

But what is humour? It is certainly not a peculiarly Christian thing. Is it then an exclusively human phenomenon? Henri Bergson, a twentieth century[11] French-Jewish philosopher, thought so. In his essay on Laughter, he wrote:

'The first point to which attention should be called is that the comic does not exist outside the pale of what is strictly HUMAN. A landscape may be beautiful, charming and sublime, or insignificant and ugly; it will never be laughable. You may laugh at an animal, but only because you have detected in it some human attitude or expression. You may laugh at a hat, but what you are making fun of, in this case, is not the piece of felt or straw, but the shape that men have given it, — the human caprice whose mould it has assumed. It is strange that so important a fact, and such a simple one too, has not attracted to a greater degree the attention of philosophers. Several have defined man as "an animal which laughs." They might equally well have defined him as an animal which is laughed at; for if any other animal, or some lifeless object, produces the same effect, it is always because of some resemblance to man, of the stamp he gives it or the use he puts it to.'[12]

Figure 1: French-Jewish philosopher Henri Bergson (1859-1941) died an unofficial Roman Catholic; Public Domain

---

11   18th October 1859 — 4th January 1941
12   Laughter — An Essay On The Meaning Of Comic, Henri Bergson ; originally published in 1900 in French as 'Le Rire. Essai Sur La Signification Du Comique'.

Bergson's essay is famous and has been described as profound. But is he right that humour is an exclusively *human* thing? That might depend upon how humour is defined. The problem of defining humour has been acknowledged as difficult since Aristotle. What combination of the following constitutes humour?

> Paradox, the Preposterous, Irony, Sarcasm, Hyperbole, Absurdity, Incongruity, Coincidence, Understatement (sometimes called Litotes or Meiosis), Insult, Taunt, Gloat, Surprise, Wit, Trickery, Juxtaposition, Ambiguity, a Joke, Slap-stick, a Pun, Word-play, a Riddle, Scorn, Shock, Teasing, Vulgarity, Recognition, Caricature, Spoof, Satire, Disbelief, Discomfort, Amazement, Incredulity, Triumph. [13]

Categories of Biblical Humour

If we make do with that list for the time being, we can certainly say that all those categories represent human experiences. We enjoy a paradox, we guffaw at the preposterous, we smile at irony, get wowed by hyperbole, and love insult (if directed at Dagon or Philistines).

But are such experiences limited to us humans? Can God experience humour? Does God express amusement or employ humour too? Passages like Psalm 2 would seem to indicate so-

- Psalm 2:4 *The One enthroned in heaven laughs;*
  the Lord scoffs at them.
  ⁵He rebukes them in his anger... NIV

Psalm 2 certainly has God *laughing* at humans; it also combines humour (*laughs*) and seriousness (*rebukes, anger*) as previously noted. But could the psalm simply be using words like '*laughs*' as a metaphor for something divine that we mere humans simply cannot understand or enter into?

Some time ago I was reading on an Internet discussion group that fatherhood is a kind of metaphor that helps us to understand, from our own experience of fatherhood, what it means for God to be our father. However, it was rapidly pointed out that this idea of fatherhood being a metaphor is completely the wrong way around, and theologically incorrect: God is the source of fatherhood; we learn from his ideal fatherhood how we, as fathers, should relate to our children[14]. This is part of us having been made

---

13 And this is hardly an exhaustive list, but it does appear to cover common kinds of humour in the Bible.

14 This is probably what Paul means in Ephesians 3:14-15 τὸν πατέρα, ¹⁵ ἐξ οὗ πᾶσα πατριὰ ἐν οὐρανοῖς καὶ ἐπὶ γῆς ὀνομάζεται = *the Father, from whom all fatherhood in heaven and on*

in his image. Inasmuch as we are good fathers, we image God. Inasmuch as we have been created in his image, and are aided by the Holy Spirit, we are able to show to the world around us what the concept of fatherhood really means.

The same must be true for humour. Humour is not something exclusively human. It cannot be used as a crude metaphor of something divine to help us understand God. Humour has its source in God.

While we humans may often be the objects of divine humour, when *the One enthroned in heaven laughs* at us, we also image[15] him when we laugh. We should not laugh at him, but we may and must laugh with him. As humans made in the image of God, we inherit[16] his penchant for laughter. We do not always employ it righteously, as when the Jews laughed at Jesus in Luke 8:53, but we do do it as a result of having been made in his *likeness[17]*.

Presumably God does not experience the element of surprise that is an essential ingredient in some humour, because he is outside time.

And what about the impassibility[18] of God? His impassibility means that no change can be forced upon him unwillingly. But all sorts of emotions can be expressed by the divine nature quite willingly, for example, love, hatred and, in Psalm 2, *anger*. We would have to be very brave[19], in the light of Psalm 2:2, and many other verses, to assert that God is incapable of humour.

But surely the real revelation of God's humour is what it looked like on the face of Jesus, and what it sounded like when he spoke. See the chapters herein on the gospels and Acts. Since Jesus is one person with two natures, one human, the other divine[20], in perfect relation to each other, then, if Jesus has humour, who would dare say that God is humourless? Indeed, Elton Trueblood has written a whole book[21] devoted to the relatively narrow subject of Jesus' own humour. Trueblood was not a Conservative Evangelical. He was a Quaker, but one who took the gospels seriously, and identified 'thirty humorous passages in the synoptic gospels'. Each passage is an example of Jesus' own humour.

---

earth derives (SBL Gk.)

15 If you are unfamiliar with the word 'image' being used as a verb, see 'Some Perspectives on the Image of God in Man from Biblical Theology', Robert C. Newman, Biblical Theological Seminary, Hatfield, Pa, IBRI, 1984.

16 Acts 17:28-29

17 Genesis 1:26; 5:1,3

18 *'Impassible', that is, incapable of suffering and death, free from ignorance, and insusceptible to weakness and temptation'* — Louis Berkhof, *Systematic Theology*, III C, 1949 reprint.

19 And perhaps heretical?

20 *Westminster Confession of Faith* 8.2, 1646/7

21 *The Humor of Christ*, Elton Trueblood, Harper & Row, 1964.

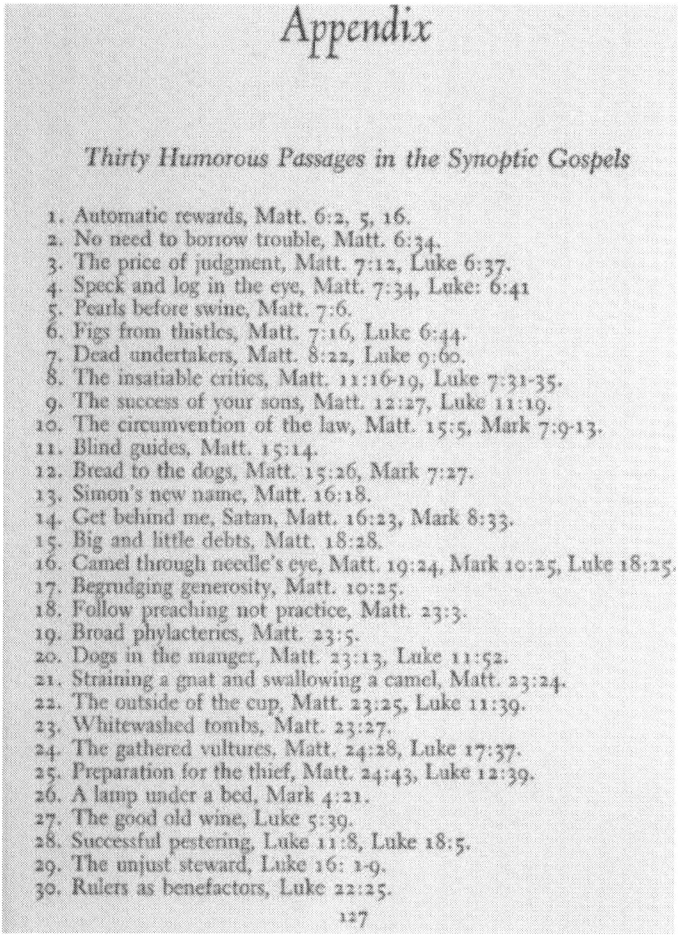

Appendix

Thirty Humorous Passages in the Synoptic Gospels

1. Automatic rewards, Matt. 6:2, 5, 16.
2. No need to borrow trouble, Matt. 6:34.
3. The price of judgment, Matt. 7:12, Luke 6:37.
4. Speck and log in the eye, Matt. 7:34, Luke: 6:41
5. Pearls before swine, Matt. 7:6.
6. Figs from thistles, Matt. 7:16, Luke 6:44.
7. Dead undertakers, Matt. 8:22, Luke 9:60.
8. The insatiable critics, Matt. 11:16-19, Luke 7:31-35.
9. The success of your sons, Matt. 12:27, Luke 11:19.
10. The circumvention of the law, Matt. 15:5, Mark 7:9-13.
11. Blind guides, Matt. 15:14.
12. Bread to the dogs, Matt. 15:26, Mark 7:27.
13. Simon's new name, Matt. 16:18.
14. Get behind me, Satan, Matt. 16:23, Mark 8:33.
15. Big and little debts, Matt. 18:28.
16. Camel through needle's eye, Matt. 19:24, Mark 10:25, Luke 18:25.
17. Begrudging generosity, Matt. 10:25.
18. Follow preaching not practice, Matt. 23:3.
19. Broad phylacteries, Matt. 23:5.
20. Dogs in the manger, Matt. 23:13, Luke 11:52.
21. Straining a gnat and swallowing a camel, Matt. 23:24.
22. The outside of the cup, Matt. 23:25, Luke 11:39.
23. Whitewashed tombs, Matt. 23:27.
24. The gathered vultures, Matt. 24:28, Luke 17:37.
25. Preparation for the thief, Matt. 24:43, Luke 12:39.
26. A lamp under a bed, Mark 4:21.
27. The good old wine, Luke 5:39.
28. Successful pestering, Luke 11:8, Luke 18:5.
29. The unjust steward, Luke 16: 1-9.
30. Rulers as benefactors, Luke 22:25.

*Figure 2: The Humor(sic) of Christ, Elton Trueblood,
Harper & Row, 1964*

And what of scripture being God-breathed?[22] Well, Psalm 2 certainly records him *laughing*. In 1 Samuel 5, *the LORD* single-handedly takes on *Dagon*. He not only hilariously defeats *Dagon*, but also breathes out the side-splitting story via the prophet Samuel for us to enjoy, learn from, and laugh at for ourselves.

But would it not be safer simply to assume that the Bible is not being humorous except in those passages where it is undeniable and totally obvious? Not really, because we have to recognise humour in scripture in order to understand it in the first place. If we fail to spot humour in a passage, we will misunderstand it. If we misunderstand it, we will also misapply it.

---

22 Theopneustos (θεόπνευστος) in 2 Timothy 3:16 means 'breathed out by God', not 'inspired'.

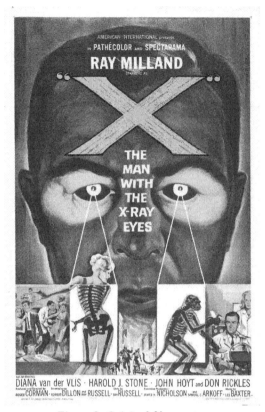

*Figure 3: Original film poster.
From wikipedia as Public Domain.*

When I was young, my irresponsible parents[23] allowed me to watch a horror film, *The Man with the X-Ray Eyes*. In the end, being able to see straight through everything drives the man into a desperate state. He finds himself in a tent meeting where the preacher misquotes (from the AV[24] — the film dates from 1963), '*If thine eye offend thee, pluck it out.*' The man with X-ray eyes does not at this point stop to perform a detailed exegesis of Jesus' words in the sermon on the mount, he immediately chooses to blind himself.

- Matthew 5:29 *If your right eye causes you to stumble, gouge it out and throw it away. It is better for you to lose one part of your body than for your whole body to be thrown into hell.* NIV

Now if he had taken the time to buy a modern translation and studied the passage in its context, and maybe looked up some commentaries, he might still have *plucked out*

---

23 That is an example of humour that is actually untrue. Biblical humour is usually true.
24 KJV 1789

his *eyes*. After all, Jesus does actually make a pretty direct connection between *eyes*, sin, and being thrown into *hell*.

However, commentators agree (I think) that the intention of Matthew 5:29 was to get Jesus' disciples to take sin seriously thereby avoiding *hell*, not actually to *pluck out* their *eyes*. In any case, a disciple who *plucked out* his *right eye as* instructed would still have his left to lead him into sin. And even a now completely sightless person would still be capable of sinning through remembered images.[25]

What Jesus did in Matthew 5:29 was to use a discomforting hyperbole to create a preposterous command followed by unassailable logic in order to grab everyone's attention. He shocked us about the seriousness of *sin*, helped us to repent of visual sins, and, by listening to this, and everything else that Jesus taught, to avoid *hell*.

But even a preposterous hyperbole about self-mutilation is actually humour of a kind. It is certainly not 'funny-ha-ha' humour, a mere joke, or slapstick, but it is a kind of gothic humour, a type sometimes employed by the apostle Paul[26] as well as by Jesus. If we react to this kind of humour by rationalising away Jesus' command, using reason based on the number of *eyes* we have, and by appealing to other commands that Jesus gave, certainly we will avoid any self-mutilation. But such, uncalled-for, complex, thought processes will also blunt the humour. A joke explained is a joke spoiled.

If however, we allow Jesus' shocking command to strike us as preposterous hyperbole, i.e. as humour of a sort, without thinking too deeply about just how he is teaching us, we will find that his use of humour enables us to take *sin* seriously. It helps us to repent, remember his teaching, and avoid *hell* without doing any eye-gouging.[27]

Similarly, what do you think about this verse?-

---

25 My point here is not that we must confidently assign this verse to a humorous category, but that we must *decide* whether it contains humour or not, and that will affect how we interpret it.

26 For example, Galatians 5:12

27 Elton Trueblood does not dare(?) to cite Matthew 5:29 as a humorous passage in *The Humor*(sic) *of Christ*, but David A. Peters does, in his *The Many Faces of Biblical Humor*(sic), Hamilton Books, 2008. Peters says that Matthew 5:29-30 is '*so ludicrous that it is absurdly funny. However, that absurdity serves to relate the reality and horror of hell*' p244. Peters' vast volume of 434 pages deals with far more passages than just the humorous ones, but clearly labels Matthew 5:29 as humorous. He has tuned in to Bible's peculiar blends of humour, but it is a pity that his Biblical quotations often use translations that would make almost any passage seem funny!

- Matthew 6:27 *Can any one of you by worrying add a single hour to your life*[a]? Footnote [a]: *Matthew 6:27 Or single cubit[28] to your height* NIV

How Jesus' question strikes us would affect not only how we understand and obey the verse, but perhaps even how a translator might translate it. He might think to himself, 'Well nobody would ever want to add 18 inches to his height; I think this must be a piece of idiom here, perhaps meaning to extend one's lifespan, not one's height'. He might then render it this way, "*add a single hour to your life*".

If, however, the translator were to think to himself, 'Add 18 inches to my height? That is preposterous; Jesus must be employing humour', he would translate it more literally, "*add a single cubit to your height*". Now without deciding finally which is the better translation, we can see from these two possibilities how important it is to recognise humour in scripture, and at the earliest possible stage in the process. Once again, it may not be funny-ha-ha humour, but it may well be humour.

*****

Let us now divide the Bible up into sections that follow the familiar Western ordering used in the contents page of most English Bibles. We will look at the amount and type of humour in the books of Moses (the Pentateuch), the history books, the wisdom books, the major and minor prophets, the gospels and the letters. It will often be humorous, and will always be serious.

2. Humour in the Pentateuch

Apart from Leviticus, the books of Moses contain lots of narrative in the form of true stories. The remaining four books are full of people doing things, saying things, and the general stuff of life 4,000 years ago. So, we would expect to find some humour, and are not disappointed.

2.1 Genesis

- Genesis 2:7 *Then the LORD God formed a man from the dust of the ground...*

Even before the fall, some gentle humour appears in the form of a pun on the word 'adam', meaning '*man*'. *The LORD God* forms an 'Adam' *from the dust of the* 'adamah'. The pun is not at all apparent in an English translation[29], of course, but is God reminding us, right at the outset of human history, that we are just *dust of the ground*. It seems a funny place to put words reminiscent of a funeral service — '*dust*

---

28 About 18 inches
29 Except through the judicious use of footnotes

to dust', but there it is, possibly the first bit of humour in the story of humanity. It is gentle; it should keep us humble, but it is definitely humour.

The fall and the flood intervene. There are more puns, but then the LORD singles out a man from whom he will build a new family that is a better family than Adam's, a better family than Noah's: Abram. Immediately, Abram is called upon to believe the unbelievable, and he does[30]. But then, in Genesis 18, some laughter appears on the lips of Abram's wife, *Sarah-*

- Genesis 18:12 *So Sarah laughed to herself as she thought,*
   'After I am worn out and my lord is old, will I now have this
   pleasure?' NIV

What kind of *laughter* is this? Is there some humour? Yes, humour of a sort. It is actually the *laughter* of disbelief. The LORD is visiting Abram to tell him, amongst other things, that next year he will have a son. There is already the smell of irony in the story, because Abram has already been renamed 'Abraham' which means father-of-many, when he only has one son[31] in his quiver[32]. And now, both Abraham and *Sarah* his wife are far too old to expect any more children[33].

The LORD asks Abraham why *Sarah laughed*. She denies it, thereby confirming that her *laughter* was mainly a matter of sinful unbelief. But the LORD insists that she did *laugh*. So, there was definitely humour; God said so, but it was not very godly humour. It was the humour of surprise seasoned with unbelief. It was a case of the amazing being greeted as merely the preposterous. We need to catch ourselves if we react to material in the Bible that seems to us to be preposterous. It is important not to confuse the amazing with the preposterous.

However, the story does not end there, because in Genesis 21, after the promised baby son has graciously been born, Abraham names him Isaac, which means 'he *laughs*'. And then-

- Genesis 21:6 *Sarah said, 'God has brought me laughter,*
   and everyone who hears about this will laugh with me.' NIV

Does *Sarah* have the last laugh? No, she ascribes the humour to *God*. Now, instead of *laughing* at *God*, she is *laughing* with him. *Sarah* has learned to

---

30   Genesis 15:6
31   Ishmael, see Genesis 16:15
32   See Psalm 127:5
33   Genesis 18:11; Hebrews 11:12

take *God* at his word, that is, seriously. Her son, named Isaac, will serve as a constant reminder to everyone that we must *laugh* with God, never at him.

In the very next chapter, the angels who visited Abraham and Sarah try to rescue Lot and his family from Sodom shortly before the LORD will destroy the city. In particular, *Lot's* prospective *sons-in-law* refuse to flee; they think he is *joking-*

- Genesis 19:14 So *Lot went out and spoke to his sons-in-law, who were pledged to marry his daughters. He said, 'Hurry and get out of this place, because the LORD is about to destroy the city!' But his sons-in-law thought he was joking.* NIV

The Hebrew word for *joking* in 19:14 is the same as for *laughing* in 21:6. But, this time, there was no *joking* or laughter, and so they suffer the fate of everyone who remained in Sodom. Here, we see the juxtapositioning of humour and severity in the Bible. In a way, the *sons-in-law* lost their lives to teach us[34] the importance of seeing humour in the word of God when it is there, and of making sure that we do not see it when it is not there.

As in the case of *Sarah laughing*, the narratives in Genesis spread the humour out over many chapters. To get the joke, take the warning, and learn the theology, we have to read large chunks of text, as is also the case with Jacob.

In Genesis 25, Jacob and Esau are born to Isaac and Rebekah. Jacob's name means something like *'he grasps the heel'* which is Hebrew idiom for 'he deceives'[35]. Thus, Jacob, the Deceiver enters the Genesis narrative. In fact, just four verses after he has been born, Jacob makes his first 'move', and cons his brother Esau out of his birthright as eldest son!

Two chapters later, Jacob the Deceiver, with the aid of his mother, cons Esau out of his blind father's patriarchal blessing. In fact, Jacob's deception of his ailing father is so elaborate that, in the end, it is only because Jacob has managed to make himself smell like Esau, that it works! His father is (wrongly) sure that he has the right son there in front of him, and blesses him. Enjoy the unbelievable story in Genesis 27. There is humour in the air, but the punchline has not been delivered yet.

It is no surprise that Jacob has to flee for his life to live with his uncle Laban, a long way North of Esau. Esau smouldered with anger at his brother for a long time. So, Jacob spends a long time with Laban, and eventually earns the hand of Laban's daughter Rachel in marriage.

---

34 1 Corinthians 10:6 *'Now these things happened as examples ...'*
35 Perhaps the story of Jacob is the origin of the idiom, not the other way around?

Such are the wedding festivities that, the morning after, Jacob wakes up and discovers that his uncle has married him off to the wrong daughter, the ugly short-sighted one! How the deceiver has been deceived. God is providentially at work in Jacob's life and heart. The LORD is giving him a dose of his own medicine-

- Genesis 29:25 *When morning came, there was Leah!* NIV

The comic surprise of Genesis 29:25 delights the reader. The painful irony when we realise who it is that has been deceived warns us, and we appreciate how God sometimes works in the lives of his covenant people nowadays too!

So far, in Genesis, we have seen the humour of puns, surprise, irony, and even the danger of misplaced humour. And when Jacob flees from Laban, we see more of the same. There are more puns based on the idea of stealing[36], but also a new kind of humour, the vulgar.

After a while of living with uncle Laban, Jacob notices that Laban's attitude to him has become less than familial. So, he convinces his wives that it is time to leave, and they depart in a hurry. Now, you know how it is when you move home: Some items belong very clearly to one or another member of the family, but there are some whose actual ownership is vague — that heirloom, that joint birthday present, that hand-me-down. Anyway, Rachel decides that she has every right to claim some of her father's teraphim gods. What are teraphim(?), you say. Here are some teraphim-

Figure 4: Ancient near Eastern teraphim (Canaanite)
wikimedia commons,
Creative Commons Attribution 4.0 International license(sic)

---

36 See the original language in 30:33; 31:19,20,26,27,30,32.

Such teraphim gods were used to ward off evil by appealing to ancestors to help the household, hence the human shapes of the statuettes. They were small and quite portable, being made of wood, stone or metal. So, in Genesis 31, Rachel, fearing for the safety of her family, steals her father's teraphim.

The only problem was that Laban came looking for them. Now Jacob had no idea what Rachel, his favourite wife, had done, so he goes on oath to Laban-

- Genesis 31:32 *"But if you find anyone who has your gods, that person shall not live. In the presence of our relatives, see for yourself whether there is anything of yours here with me; and if so, take it."* NIV

The air is thick with irony. Rachel is now not only a thief but also under threat of death, so what can Jacob's favourite wife do?

She sits on them and claims to be having her period!

It works, and Laban goes home again. Can you see what the author, Moses, has done here? He has written Genesis in the context of the people of Israel, with all their laws and regulations about blood and about human emissions[37], which are connected with uncleanness and sin. He has then used Rachel's quick thinking to insult Laban's teraphim gods in quite a vulgar way!

I once preached on this passage on a Sunday morning. After the service, a young lady came up to me to castigate me. She said that there was nothing unclean or sinful about periods, bodily emissions or blood. And in one sense she was quite right. But she was failing to enter the thought world of Moses' original readers, who would immediately have seen the humour in Laban's idols being anointed with bodily fluids. The teraphim are helpless; they are (now) unclean. How ridiculous to trust such godlets to save your household!

Indeed, by the time Jacob and his household arrive back in the promised land and meet the deceived Esau, Jacob, whose name is now *Israel*[38], is confidently trusting the real God, not teraphim, as witnessed by Jacob's new altar and its name-

- Genesis 33:20 *There he set up an altar and called it El Elohe Israel.*
  Footnote: *El Elohe Israel* can mean *El is the God of Israel* or *mighty is the God of Israel.* NIV

---

37 e.g. Leviticus 15:20
38 As given by God in Genesis 32:28

What are you trusting in to bless your family? Is it money, education, a healthy diet, medical care, a pension? You need to laugh at these 21st Century teraphim and trust the *God of Israel*.

2.3 Exodus

In many ways, Exodus is similar to Leviticus in its sobriety, but Exodus does contain quite a lot of narrative, so we would expect to find some humour. In Exodus 7:8-13, Moses and Aaron confront Pharaoh with the power of *the LORD*-

- Exodus 7:10 *So Moses and Aaron went to Pharaoh and did just as the LORD commanded. Aaron threw his staff down in front of Pharaoh and his officials, and it became a snake.* NIV

Perhaps *Aaron* is demonstrating his dominance over the Egyptian snake goddess, Wadjet[39], a cobra? Unfortunately (not), that one back-fires when Pharaoh's magicians manage to duplicate the miracle. But nothing is 'unfortunate' in God's economy: Pharaoh's heart becomes hard, and the stage is now set for a 'shoot-out' between the one true God and the many fake gods of Egypt.

*Figure 5: Hapi the Nile god,
Encyclopaedia Biblica,
c.1903, now public domain*

---

39 It is difficult to be certain of the identities of many Egyptian gods, but some, like Hapi, the Nile god, are obvious.

The first godlet to be killed is Hapi[40], the Nile god, whom *the LORD* changes overnight into a stinking, useless, dead god (Exodus 7:18). We know he is dead because the Nile is filled with blood. Now, sitting at home, in your comfortable armchair, sipping the beverage of your choice, that may not seem very humorous. But if, instead, you had been under the threat of genocide whilst being abused by Egyptian slave masters, as the Jews had been, you would certainly find such a divine defeat amusing. Unless, of course, you too had been worn down by many decades of paganism, and were now worshipping the same gods as the Egyptians! This demonstrates the importance of the ten plagues: They were meant to convince everyone, but especially the suffering Jews, that *the LORD* was the only true God.

And so, the plagues continue, as one god after another is defeated by *the LORD*: The frog or toad goddess (Exodus 8), Heket is defeated; Heket again (Exodus 8:13), this time as the dead frog goddess who was meant to protect women in childbirth; Geb, the god of the earth (i.e. 'dust', as per Exodus 8:16).

Figure 6: Heket the frog god, from wikipedia

Khepri, the god with a head of a fly, is defeated in Exodus 8:20-24. When hail rains down in Exodus 9:13-35, crops are destroyed, and thunder claps. Everywhere, except where the Israelites are, is in tatters. The Egyptians are given a warning so that they can decide whose side they are on, and a few (verse 20) take notice, but all the others leave their slaves and livestock outside to be killed. And so it goes on until Egypt is ruined (Exodus 10:7), and all Egypt's gods have been defeated. It is all seriously and sadly humorous. The humour is at the expense of Pharaoh and his gods, so that *the LORD* will get all the glory (Exodus 14:4, 17, 18; 15:11).

****

Not much of the humour in Exodus is laugh-out-loud humour, but there is one incident that definitely is. Discomfortingly, it comes at the absolute spiritual low point of the story. Moses had been gone for a long time, but less than forty days, in

---
40 Sadly, the obvious pun only really works in English.

order to receive the law from *the LORD*, including the ten commandments which contain the explicit prohibition-

- Exodus 20:4 '*You shall not make for yourself an image in the form of anything in heaven above or on the earth beneath or in the waters below. ⁵ You shall not bow down to them or worship them; ...*' NIV

Giving in to the people's impatience and some polytheistic pagan peer pressure, Aaron makes them a golden calf to *worship, an image.* Now maybe he is aiming for a compromise, so that the people will still worship *the LORD*, but do it through bowing down to a golden calf that somehow represents the true God. That could be why he says to the people-

- Exodus 32:4b '*... This is your god[41], Israel, who brought you up out of Egypt...*
  ⁵⁻⁻⁻ *Tomorrow there will be a festival to the LORD.*'

But any true lover of *the LORD* reads Exodus 32:1-23 with only horror at what Aaron and the people have done: Explicit idolatry while Moses is on the mountain receiving the ten commandments! So when Moses reappears, having smashed the stone tablets containing the very command that Aaron has just broken[42], he is incandescent with rage, grinds the calf to powder, and makes the people drink water polluted by the calf-dust. In Exodus 32:21, he confronts his brother Aaron, who immediately tries to blame everyone but himself-

- Exodus 32:24b '*... Then they gave me the gold, I threw it into the fire, and out came this calf!*' NIV

...as if by magic. Humour? At this abjectly serious stage of the story? Presumably Moses just recorded Aaron's words verbatim in verse 24, but yes, here is humour on the lips of Aaron at the epicentre of his failure, faithfully recorded in scripture by the prophet Moses.

Well, no reader will forget that. The bitter shame of idolatry, sweetly iced with Aaron's absurd excuse, stands out as the most incongruous verse in Exodus.

---

41 It is '*god*' singular, because the original Hebrew often uses plurals to indicate greatness, majesty, grandeur or holiness, not to indicate actual plurality, as in this case. There was, after all, just the one golden calf. Some commentators have speculated that the plural is there to imply polytheism, but this seems an unnecessary complication. See p5 of *The Pluralis Intensivus in Hebrew*, Aaron(!) Ember, Baltimore MD dissertation, 1906.

42 Again, one supposes that this is the origin of the concept of breaking the law in scripture and in normal English usage.

As we add the categories of 'Absurdity' and 'Incongruity' to our list[43] of types of biblical humour, no doubt there are life lessons here about not giving in to peer pressure or you might look as sinfully-stupid as Aaron. But the true believer will immediately be glad that he has a far better high priest than Aaron-

- Hebrews 7:26 *Such a high priest truly meets our need– one who is holy, blameless, pure, set apart from sinners, exalted above the heavens.* NIV

2.3 Leviticus

Leviticus seems to be devoid of humour. Here Moses deals with the subject of God's holiness. Perhaps nobody wise would risk using humour on a subject like that, not even Aaron.

2.4 Numbers

Numbers 22 to 24 contain the story of *Balaam*, a prophet who seems to be a genuine prophet, even though he is not a member of *God's* people in any sense[44]. He is an enemy of *God's* people[45] who is used by the LORD to bless them, but that was not his intention, nor the intention of the Moabite king, Balak, who hired him do some divination and curse the Israelites.

Towards the start of the story, *Balaam* is forbidden to go and curse Israel-

- Numbers 22:12 *But God said to Balaam, 'Do not go with them. You must not put a curse on those people, because they are blessed.'* NIV

God's people are not just those who have been *blessed* at some point in the past, it is part of their identity; they simply *are blessed*.

But *Balaam* smells the scent of money and gets on his *donkey*. En route, the *donkey* sees the angel of the LORD, and swerves, inviting a beating from *Balaam*, to which the *donkey* replies-

- Numbers 22:30 … *'Am I not your own donkey, which you have always ridden, to this day? Have I been in the habit of doing this to you?'*

The rhyme comes to mind-

---

43   See the categories of humour box in the introduction.
44   Matthew 7:22 is relevant.
45   Revelation 2:14

The god of thunder was outside, a-seated on his filly.
  "I'm Thor", he cried;
  The horse replied-
"Thorgot your thaddle thilly".[46]

Figure 7: Balaam by Rembrandt, from Wikimedia commons,
Creative Commons Attribution-
Share Alike 4.0 International licence

The fact that *Balaam* does not immediately freak out at being spoken to by a dumb *donkey*[47] is a signal to us that some biblical humour is afoot. Something ridiculous and amazing is taking place; a *donkey* is revealing to its master that the master has less insight than the *donkey*. In short, Balaam's *donkey* is making an ass of him. The professional *seer* cannot *see*

---
46 Of unknown and dubious provenance
47 For American readers, '*dumb*' means unable to speak.

the angel of the LORD! The prophesying is done by his animal! He cannot even control his *donkey*, never mind curse God's *blessed* people. Peter confirms how absurd the situation is-

- 2 Peter 2:16 *But he* [Balaam] *was rebuked for his wrongdoing by a donkey — an animal without speech — who spoke with a human voice and restrained the prophet's madness.*

But the humour does not end there; King Balak requires some ridicule too. *Balaam* utters seven oracles for him, and all of them fail to curse the Israelites. But full marks to Balak for persistence. First, he offers some sacrifices, to whom or what we do not know. Then he takes *Balaam* to where he can see just the edge of Israelite encampment. In chapter 23, more offerings are made, perhaps to the LORD this time, and the LORD puts into *Balaam's* mouth his first oracle-

- Numbers 23:8 [Balaam:] *"How can I curse those whom God has not cursed?"*

Well, that could have gone better. So Balak tries varying the view of Israel, and more animals are sacrificed-

- Numbers 23:21 [Balaam:] *"No misfortune is seen in Jacob,*
  no misery observed in Israel."

And so it goes on all through chapter 24; *Balaam* just cannot seem to curse Israel. He manages to curse the Moabites, Edomites, Amalekites, Kenites, Cypriots, Ashur and Eber (24:17-24). The first of those is particularly embarrassing, because Balak is king of the Moabites! A smile must surely be playing on the divine lips by now. *Balaam* even manages to predict the coming of the Messiah-

- Numbers 24:17 '*I see him, but not now;*
  I behold him, but not near.
  A star will come out of Jacob;
  a sceptre will rise out of Israel.' NIV

And in this way the LORD makes an ass not only out of *Balaam*, but also out of his benefactor, Balak. And just in case you wondered ...

- Numbers 31:7 *They* [Israel] *fought against Midian, as the LORD commanded Moses, ...8... They also killed Balaam son of Beor with the sword.*

So if you belong to *the LORD*, it doesn't matter how unworthy[48] you feel or what sins beset you[49], nobody can ever curse you. In Christ, you are fundamentally *blessed*. All things work together for your good[50].

2.5 Deuteronomy

Deuteronomy introduces a new kind of humour, rather an unpleasant sort: Taunting. In Deuteronomy 32:27 Moses is reciting a song to the Israelites in which he expresses *dread* that the enemies of God's people might '*taunt*' them-

- Deuteronomy 32:27 "*but I dreaded the taunt of the enemy,*
    lest the adversary misunderstand
 and say, "Our hand has triumphed[51];
    the LORD has not done all this." NIV

Here, there is the fear that the Gentiles might think they have triumphed over Israel when, in fact, judgement on his unfaithful people is something that *the LORD* alone has performed. Why will God judge his people himself? Because they will break all his laws.

Deuteronomy is broadly an exposition of the ten commandments found in chapter 5[52]. Chapters 30 and 31 predict the people's failure to keep God's laws, so his judgement is inevitable. It is just, and it will be carried out with the attendant risk that the Gentiles will see it and come to the wrong conclusion, that they, themselves, were victorious over Israel. *Taunting* is humour too.

The same song has *the LORD* himself taunting the idolatrous Israelites and asking the ironic question-

- Deuteronomy 32:37 ...'*Now where are their gods,*
    the rock they took refuge in,
  [38] the gods who ate the fat of their sacrifices
    and drank the wine of their drink offerings?
  Let them rise up to help you!
    Let them give you shelter!' NIV

---

48 Genesis 32:10; Job 40:4; Luke 17:10
49 And the ancient Israelites certainly knew a thing or two about besetting sins.
50 Romans 8:28
51 See the section on Psalms for more on the subject of *triumph*.
52 See, for example: Deuteronomy — The Commands of a covenant God, Allan Harman, CF, 2001.

It is all right, even good and healthy, to laugh ironically at idols, but we should dread people laughing at the true God. How much of the behaviour of Christians, when we fall out with each other, might lead people to laugh at us and at our God?

3. Humour in the History Books

3.1 Joshua

By the time Joshua becomes leader, the promised land is being parcelled out to the tribes of Israel. But the book of Joshua is a hard read for modern people with all its genocide, divine justice, and long boring lists of who got what where within the *land flowing with milk and honey[53]*. Is there room for any humour in such a chilling book?

One of the refrains in Joshua is, *'Be strong and courageous!'*. It is said by the LORD to Joshua, by Joshua to the people, and then echoed back by the people in the first chapter (1:6,7,9,18). Why was such repetition needed? Simply because the people had been weak and timid, leading to their forty years of wandering around the wilderness. This weakness and timidity was not merely a lack of strength and courage, it was a spiritual failure. It was not just low morale, but sin, The people had not trusted God, but had feared the Anakites[54], and had refused to go and conquer the promised land.

None of that is at all humorous. But in Joshua 2, the LORD works in the heart of a pagan prostitute to give the Israelites a living, breathing, humorous, object lesson in trusting God: Rahab. When the Israelite *spies* enter her house in Jericho, the local king finds out about it and says-

- Joshua 2:3 ...*'Bring out the men who came to you and entered your house, because they have come to spy out the whole land.'* NIV

In that moment, Rahab has to decide whether she is going to trust, and be loyal to, the moon god that they probably all worshipped around then in Jericho, or do something else. Surprisingly, she decides on 'do something else': She hides the *spies* and lies[55] about it! Why oh why would she do something as risky as that? She explains-

- Joshua 2:9 *'I know that the LORD has given this land to you and that a great fear of you has fallen on us, so that all who live in this country are melting in fear because of you. [10] We have heard how the LORD dried up the water of the Red Sea for you when you came out of Egypt, and what you did to Sihon and Og, the two*

---

53 Joshua 5:6
54 Perhaps giants, as per Exodus 13:33.
55 It really should not surprise us that a pagan prostitute might lie.

kings of the Amorites east of the Jordan, whom you completely destroyed. ^{11} *When we heard of it, our hearts sank and everyone's courage failed because of you, for the* LORD *your God is God in heaven above and on the earth below.'* NIV

Rahab had heard just a fleeting summary, a rumour, of what *the LORD* was like and what he had done, and that he had promised to give Jericho, her home, to the Israelites. And at that moment, she decisively puts her trust in *the LORD* alone.

And here is the joke: The Israelites, who had been protected by *the LORD* for forty years, brought miraculously *out of Egypt*, taught the whole law of God by Moses, struggled to trust and obey. But this despised, pagan, prostitute, who had only heard rumours of what God was like, put them all to shame by being *strong and courageous* (1:6-9,18; 10:25).

As Hebrews puts it-

- Hebrews 11:31 *By faith the prostitute Rahab, because she welcomed the spies, was not killed with those who were disobedient…*

… and became an ancestor of Jesus.[56] But most of all, she shames all the readers of the book of Joshua who struggle to trust God. Now that is biblical humour.

****

Later on, Joshua 14:10 may be a miracle, but is more likely to be just some 85-year-old hyperbole-

- Joshua 14:10 [Caleb:] *'Now then, just as the* LORD *promised, he has kept me alive for forty-five years since the time he said this to Moses, while Israel moved about in the wilderness. So here I am today, eighty-five years old!* ^{11} *I am still as strong today as the day Moses sent me out; I'm just as vigorous to go out to battle now as I was then…'* NIV

Was Caleb really as fit as he had been aged forty? It is possible, by God's power. But it seems more likely that God, in his providence, rather than by a miracle, had kept Caleb relatively healthy to vindicate Caleb's faithfulness, and to show that God keeps his promises even over long periods of time. In which case, Caleb's statement about still being *as strong as* he was *forty-five years* ago is probably hyperbole, a sort of humour, but used in all seriousness to claim his share of the promised land.

---

56 Matthew 1:5. Now we also know why Boaz (in Ruth 4:21) was such a godly man: His mother was Rahab.

Caleb's warm humour highlights his own faithfulness, but the way it is written also emphasises God's constancy, and his use of human vessels who are often feeble[57], but not always. If God wants us to do something, even something difficult, like defeating Anakites[58], he will provide the strength, the health, the resources, or whatever we need[59]. Where he commands, he also provides[60].

3.2 Judges

A summary of the book of Judges would be something like this: Things start off badly and only get worse. Occasional encouragements happen whenever the LORD sends a godly leader, but mostly, it is downhill all the way. Israel badly needs a *king*, but not the kind of king that *Abimelek* was in Judges 9-

- Judges 9:5 *He* [Abimelek] *went to his father's home in Ophrah and on one stone murdered his 70 brothers, the sons of Gideon. But Jotham, the youngest son of Gideon, escaped by hiding. ⁶ Then all the citizens … gathered ... to crown Abimelek king.*

The sole survivor, *Jotham*, then tells everyone present a satirical story-

- Judges 9:7b *'Listen to me, citizens of Shechem, so that God may listen to you. ⁸ One day the trees went out to anoint a king for themselves. They said to the olive tree, "Be our king."*

  ⁹ 'But the olive tree answered, "Should I give up my oil, by which both gods and humans are honoured, to hold sway over the trees?"

  ¹⁰ 'Next, the trees said to the fig-tree, "Come and be our king."

  ¹¹ 'But the fig-tree replied, "Should I give up my fruit, so good and sweet, to hold sway over the trees?"

  ¹² 'Then the trees said to the vine, "Come and be our king."

  ¹³ 'But the vine answered, "Should I give up my wine, which cheers both gods and humans, to hold sway over the trees?"

  ¹⁴ 'Finally all the trees said to the thorn-bush, "Come and be our king."

---

57 II Corinthians 4:7
58 Perhaps giants, as per Exodus 13:33. This does not appear to be a joke in scripture, merely an excuse.
59 Philippians 4:18-20
60 Genesis 22:1-14

[15] *'The thorn-bush said to the trees, "If you really want to anoint me king over you, come and take refuge in my shade; but if not, then let fire come out of the thorn-bush and consume the cedars of Lebanon!"'* NIV

The satirical story turns out to be a prophecy of judgement on the people of *Shechem* and on *Abimelek*[61]. A thousand die in a fire in the 'tower of *Shechem*'[62], and *Abimelek* himself becomes a rather unpleasant kind of laughing-stock when-

- Judges 9:53 *a woman dropped an upper millstone on his head and cracked his skull.* NIV

This was the ultimate humiliation for a warrior, so he gets his armour bearer to put him out of his misery. This is not 21st Century European humour!

What is the point of the satirical story and gothic humour surrounding the many deaths, including the death of *Abimelek*? The satirical story partly allows *Jotham* a bit of time to run away while his hearers digest the story, of course. But it also prepares the reader to laugh at *Abimelek* when he meets his grisly end.

Furthermore, the whole account provides a commentary, through satire, gothic humour, and shocking events, on human folly, the pride of warriors[63], and the danger of appointing a king whom the LORD has not appointed. You would think that such a story would really stick in the memories of the Israelites, and that none of them would want to make a similar mistake. But no, something resonant happens as soon as 1 Samuel 8 to 10, when another bad king is sought and found.

How we Christians badly need to resist acting without God's sanction, appointing without God's blessing, reasoning without God's word. We need to make sure that we look at everything through the lens of scripture, and then keep in step with him.

- Galatians 5:25 *Since we live by the Spirit, let us keep in step with the Spirit.* NIV

****

Not only does a donkey make an ass out of Balaam in Numbers 22, as we saw, but Samson also makes asses of 1,000 Philistines in Judges 15. After the violence is over, Samson says-

---

61 Verse 20
62 Judges 9:49
63 It is rather like the recurring theme of 'Klingon honour' in Star Trek.

- Judges 15:16 ..."*With an ass' jawbone*
  I have made asses of them;
  With an ass' jawbone
  I have killed 1,000 men."

In modern statistics, the deaths of even just 1,000 people are counted as a war[64]. Here we have a war overlaid by some grotesque biblical humour. Surely there is nothing funny about war, is there? No, except when the enemies of God's people are defeated in the power of the Spirit (15:14). I suspect that if we have not lived through a war personally, we do not readily appreciate such combative humour.

Samson is also quite fond of a good *riddle*; see Judges 14:12-19. But in general, and with the exception of the book of Proverbs and a few other places, the Bible does not deal in *riddles*, as the LORD says about Moses-

- Numbers 12:8 *With him I speak face to face, clearly and <u>not</u> in riddles*;

****

The book of Judges is not only full of puns and word-plays[65], but contains what David Murrow calls '*gross out*' stories[66]. These include an assassination by tent peg in Judges 4, and the particularly enjoyable account of Ehud and Eglon in Judges 3. Murrow says that unless we tackle these stories in readings, sermons and Sunday school[67], we will soon lose the interest of pre-adolescent boys; *Harry Potter*$_{TM}$ just seems so much more appealing. And part of the appeal is the gory humour.

In Judges 3, the initial humour is trickery on the part of *Ehud*, enabled by the LORD, who created him left-handed. This means that his sword is on the wrong side when he gets frisked by Eglon's lax attendants, and so he is able to get very close to the defenceless Moabite king.

Ehud says-

- Judges 3:19 ...'*Your majesty, I have a secret message for you.*' NIV

The sarcasm builds with the suspense, as we readers wonder what exactly this '*secret message*' is. Finally, Ehud delivers his *message* using his barely concealed *sword*-

- Judges 3:21 *Ehud reached with his left hand, drew the sword from his right thigh and plunged it into the king's belly.* ^{22} *Even the handle sank in after the blade, and*

---

64 And I am not minimising the tragedy of war. For background, see
https://en.wikipedia.org/wiki/List_of_wars_by_death_toll accessed 25/06/2019
65 See Judges — Such a Great Salvation, Dale Ralph Davis, CF, 2003 reprint, p57ff.
66 *Why Men Hate Going To Church,* David Murrow, Nelson Books, 2005, p179
67 See my Covenants for Evangelicals, Part II, 17.7 on Sunday School.

his bowels discharged. Ehud did not pull the sword out, and the fat closed in over it. NIV

If we didn't know what *'gross out'* meant, we do now. And it is all part of the humour: It is witty, shocking, vulgar, tricky and sarcastic. If it happened during a Sunday service, we would not laugh, but if the LORD had just delivered us from a particularly obnoxious enemy, we might.

3.3 Ruth

Ruth starts off with sadness as *Naomi* the Jewess' husband and sons all die in the land of Moab. There are word-plays, as *Naomi* says-

- Ruth 1:20 *'Don't call me **Naomi**,'* [meaning **pleasant**] *she told them. 'Call me **Mara**,* [meaning **bitter**] *because the Almighty has made my life very **bitter**. ²¹ I went away full* [as a wife with two sons], *but the* LORD *has brought me back empty. Why call me **Naomi**?'*

Here, a sad type of humour is being used to emphasise not just defeat of enemies, nor even bloody victory over idols, but to pinpoint the exact tragedy that has shaped *Naomi's* life and return to the promised land. Even the name of where she is coming back from is marked by a word-play; *Moab* means something like 'from father', reminding both Moabites and all their enemies of Moab's shameful origin in Genesis 19[68].

But despite the initial sadness, *Naomi* finds a home with Boaz and Ruth in chapter 4. The mood lifts with their domestic happiness, the punchline being the genealogy right at the end, which shows the happy family, a few generations on, producing none other than King David. What? King David is descended from miserable *Mara* and those incestuous Moabites! There is something highly amusing going on in God's providence!

Matthew, in his gospel then has the last laugh. He includes a genealogy in chapter one which only amplifies the level of humour caused by God's biological and reproductive providences. The Messiah, it turns out, is not just descended from *Moab* (Matthew 1:5), but even from a pagan prostitute, Rahab (Matthew 1:5)!

There is a lot more that can be said about that genealogy, including further humorous observations. But it has to be noted, as we leave Ruth in her domestic bliss, that the saviour identified so strongly with the people that he came to save, that he even allowed himself to be descended from the

---

68 See Genesis 19:30-38, where incest results in the birth of the two nations, Moab and Ammon.

despised, pagan, incestuous and sexually immoral. This should humble us, but also cause a wry smile to play on the lips of the redeemed.

3.4 I and II Samuel

We dealt with the hilarious humiliation of *Dagon* in the introduction, but there is more to that story; previously, Judges 16 had left some critical business unfinished-

- Judges 16:23 *Now the rulers of the Philistines assembled to offer a great sacrifice to Dagon their god and to celebrate, saying, 'Our god has delivered Samson, our enemy, into our hands.'* NIV

Now *that* is a problem. There is no way that biblical references to *Dagon* could be left hanging, for ever, with *Dagon* appearing to be omnipotent! Furthermore, when the ark of the covenant is stolen by the uncircumcised *Philistines* in 1 Samuel 5, it is at a low point amongst the people of the true God. Eli is a terrible high priest (2:30); Eli's sons are even worse (2:34) and all three of them are going to be removed, i.e. die, to be replaced by Samuel. But that does not mean that, when the ark is stolen by the *Philistines*, the uncircumcised will get any blessing from its God. Such slot-machine spirituality does not work.

Figure 8: Death mask from Philistine slipper coffin, British Museum, photo D.W. Legg 2004

I was once the treasurer of a church in Hounslow West at a time when the HMRC[69] were looking for some accounts to audit. First, they lighted on another church in Hounslow, who immediately performed a 'Jedi mind trick', and said, *"These aren't the accounts you're looking for[70]; why don't you try Hounslow West?"*

Well, something similar happens in 1 Samuel 5, when the Philistines realise that the citizens of Ashdod are all going to be either ill or dead soon if they don't get rid of the ark of the LORD. So, they try to move it to Gath (5:8), but straight away, people start falling like nine-pins. The Gathites try to move it to Ekron whose terrified residents intercept it at their city gates, insisting that the ark be repatriated to Israel. Then we read this-

- 1 Samuel 5:12 *Those who did not die were afflicted with tumours, and the outcry of the city went up to heaven.* NIV

It seems then that the Philistines are crying out to the LORD for mercy. Indeed, the Philistines seem somehow more aware of God, and in closer contact with him, than Israel are[71]. They are desperate to do the right thing with his ark. The ironic contrast with the people of Israel is stark.

The story is written in such a way that we feel sorry for these benighted Philistines who are dying like flies, and only want to do the right thing before this foreign God who is afflicting them. In this way, the account mixes pathos with irony. Both the Philistines and the Israelites seem pathetic before the ark; it is only a box, after all. If this is what his box can do, what must the God of Israel himself be like? So, they find a cunning way to send the ark back to Israel, such that it must be the case that an obvious miracle occurs, thereby justifying the accompanying offering and mode of transport (6:7-9).

They separate some cows from their calves and have them tow the ark back down the road to Israel. Their ridiculous offering of golden rats and tumours, to match their diseases and the number of their cities, are placed on a cart. The cart is drawn, pathetically, by cows, mooing all the way to *Beth Shemesh*, as the poor Philistines hope to highest *heaven* (5:12) for mercy from Israel's God. They seem to have much more of a clue about sin against a holy God than Israel have.

---

69 UK tax inspectors: "Her Majesty's Revenue and Customs"
70 "These aren't the droids you're looking for." — Obi-Wan Kenobi in Star Wars Episode IV 'A New Hope' TM
71 Just read the end of Judges and the start of 1 Samuel to convince yourself of Israel's low spiritual ebb.

This sad irony is emphasised when the sacrilegious residents of *Beth Shemesh* casually peer into the ark, as explicitly forbidden in Exodus, and 70 of them die (6:19). But the Philistines, who knew nothing about the Mosaic laws saying that the ark should only be carried by Levites and only using poles (Exodus 25:14), were shown mercy by the God of an ungodly people. The account is thick with irony, pathos, incongruity and discomfort — maybe not our favourite forms of humour; we even feel sorry for the cows (6:12), but it very much matches what passes for biblical humour.

As the people of God, we have his word, the Bible; we should always know better than our neighbours. Now and then, the heathen amongst whom we live put us to shame when-

— A *Rahab* trusts God[72], but we wobble;

— A *Ruth* stakes her life on God's mercy[73], while we rely on our salaries, pensions or the NHS[74]; or

— Some *Philistines* at least *try* to do the right thing, thereby exposing our laziness, lack of love, missing zeal, or lack of apparent need for forgiveness and humility before our God.

Most shockingly, though, it looks as if *Dagon* has the last laugh!-

- 1 Chronicles 10:8 … *the Philistines...*[9]*... proclaim the news among their idols and their people. [10] They put his* [dead King Saul's] *armour in the temple of their gods and hung up his head in the temple of Dagon.*

That can't be how the *Dagon* story ends, can it? No[75], but we need to allow the constant threat of modern *Dagons* getting the glory to galvanise our faith and zeal to serve God as God instructs us, not just as we think best.

****

That may not be how the story of *Dagon* ends[75], but it is certainly how the story of King Saul ends. Before his grisly end[76], Saul has to learn sober lessons about how-

- 1 Samuel 15:22c … *"To obey is better than sacrifice"* NIV

and

---

72 Joshua 2
73 Ruth 1:16
74 UK National Health Service, once described as *the closest thing the UK has to a national religion!*
75 Keep reading.
76 1 Samuel 31

- 1 Samuel 16:7c *"People look at the outward appearance,
  but the LORD looks at the heart."* NIV

Athough the lessons are sober, the way in which we find out Saul's inadequacies is often humorous. In 1 Samuel 9, Saul is immediately associated with the subject of *'donkeys'*. We should be expecting humour when *donkeys* are mentioned, after all that happened to Balaam in Numbers 22.[77]

In 1 Samuel 9:6, it is Saul's servant who alone shows any spiritual awareness by suggesting that they ask the local 'seer' about the missing *donkeys* that belonged to Saul's father. In the next verse, Saul is shown not only to be unspiritual but also unprepared: He has to borrow some change from the servant to pay the seer! They have carelessly run out of food. We don't suppose that that was the servant's fault, because we are now tuning in to the humour of the story, which is entirely at Saul's expense.

When they finally find the seer, who is the prophet Samuel, Saul asks the man for directions to himself(!), not realising that this man was Samuel, the local seer! It seems that Saul is always cack-handed in some way. But while we are still tittering, Samuel drops the divine bombshell[78]-

- 1 Samuel 10:1 *"Has not the Lord anointed you ruler over his
  inheritance?"* NIV

What? This nincompoop is to be king over God's people? You cannot be serious!

The *donkey* references continue into chapter 10, and when the time comes for Saul to be crowned king, he is nowhere to be found (10:21). In fact, the ridiculous situation is only resolved by means of a divine revelation-

- 1 Samuel 10:22b ... *the LORD said, 'Yes, he has hidden himself among
  the supplies.'* NIV

So, all in all, it is not surprising that this first proper king of Israel turns out to be a false start. They got what they wanted, but God could see their evil motives, and exposed them by giving them what they asked for, rather than what they needed, a king like David, a man after God's own heart[79]. An important, worrying, and profoundly spiritual story is narrated using continual humour.

---

77 See the earlier section herein on the book of Numbers.
78 And we have to pretend that we are reading the story for the first time for the shock to register properly.
79 Acts 13:22

The rest of 1 and 2 Samuel contains puns and word-plays, for example, *Nabal's* name and behaviour being linked by the underlying meaning of his name — *'fool'* (1 Samuel 25:25). But most of the narrative is sober, as we approach David's major sin with Bathsheba, and civil war with Absalom (2 Samuel 13-20). The whole book[80] centres on the verse already referred to; and how we need to make it our own-

- 1 Samuel 16:7bc "… *The* LORD *does not look at the things people look at. People look at the outward appearance, but the* LORD *looks at the heart."* NIV

3.5 I and II Kings

Donkeys are harnessed for a more noble purpose from now on. If a *donkey* served to deride Saul as a bad king, it is also true that a *donkey* is used to mark out an initially good king. So, when there is doubt about who should succeed David as king, he puts his chosen son on the royal *donkey*[81], to ride it through Jerusalem, the royal city-

- 1 Kings 1:38 *So* [they] *put Solomon on King David's mule, and they escorted him to Gihon*[82]. *39 Zadok the priest took the horn of oil from the sacred tent and anointed Solomon. Then they sounded the trumpet and all the people shouted, 'Long live King Solomon!'* NIV

And when the Messiah king is prophesied by Zechariah, he too is distinguished by approaching the royal capital on a *donkey*-

- Zechariah 9:9 *Rejoice greatly, Daughter Zion! Shout, Daughter Jerusalem! See, your king comes to you, righteous and victorious, lowly and riding on a donkey, on a colt, the foal of a donkey.*

Finally, king Jesus himself rides into Jerusalem on a *donkey* (Matthew 21:5). *Donkeys* have well and truly lost their humorous association! We may laugh at bad kings, but not at the Son of God.

When we arrive in 1 Kings 9, Solomon is now securely king, and sitting on David's throne. The LORD appears to him and confirms the Davidic Covenant[83] with him, except that this time[84], the LORD emphasises the covenant warnings and curses. One such warning is a threat that if Solomon worships idols…-

---

80 1 and 2 Samuel are a single book with no actual division between the two parts. The same is true of Kings and Chronicles, but not of Ezra-Nehemiah or Luke-Acts. The five books of Psalms have a more complex history.

81 Strictly, a *mule*

82 A spring in Jerusalem, not to be confused with a River in Genesis 2:13.

83 For more on the Davidic Covenant, see my book, 'Covenants for Evangelicals', 2019, https://www.amazon.co.uk/Covenants-Evangelicals-Understanding-Biblical-Century/dp/1090843550/

84 The previous time was in 2 Samuel 7.

- 1 Kings 9:7 *then I will cut off Israel from the land I have given them and will reject this temple I have consecrated for my Name. Israel will then become a byword and an object of ridicule among all peoples.* NIV

So here, humour is being used as a threat; it is a warning of becoming *a byword*, of *ridicule*. Not only is God's reputation at stake when we sin, so is our own.

****

Later in 1 Kings, the ridicule and taunting for the sin of idolatry comes from the prophet *Elijah*, and therefore from the LORD himself. Baal seems to be unable to light the sacrificial fire, unable to demonstrate that he is a god, so-

- 1 Kings 18:27 *At noon Elijah began to taunt them. 'Shout louder!' he said. 'Surely he* [Baal] *is a god! Perhaps he is deep in thought, or busy, or travelling. Maybe he is sleeping and must be awakened.'*

Dale Ralph Davis points out that pagan gods were often quite legitimately *busy*[85]; they led full and colourful lives. Furthermore, being *busy* might well be a humorous way of referring discreetly to a normal bodily function! Maybe he is on holiday or asleep; these are all only to be expected if the priests of Baal have constructed *a god* in their own image!

But then, although the account is simply being truthful and accurate, it becomes both gothic and pathetic at the same time-

- 1 Kings 18:28 *So they shouted louder and slashed themselves with swords and spears, as was their custom, until their blood flowed. [29] Midday passed, and they continued their frantic prophesying until the time for the evening sacrifice. But there was no response, no one answered, no one paid attention.*[86] NIV

Enough of that. Elijah repairs the altar of the LORD, saturates everything repeatedly with water, and the LORD demonstrates that he alone is God by sending fire from heaven. Monotheism works today, too.

****

Elijah's successor, Elisha, does not seem to have much of a sense of humour when, in 2 Kings 2 he is taunted for his baldness, he *curses* the jeering yobs-

---

85 The Wisdom and the Folly, CF, 2002, p239
86 A Bible translation should attempt to convey the humour of the situation or, at least, not obscure it.

- 2 Kings 2:24 *He turned round, looked at them and called down a curse on them in the name of the LORD. Then two bears came out of the woods and mauled forty-two of the boys.* NIV

That seems severe! But then we remember that Elisha is *the LORD's* representative, and that we do not laugh at *the LORD*, nor at anything connected with him. We also then recall how Elisha is a type[87] of Christ. Thus, humour is used to teach us the folly of despising the only one who can save us.

A more readily palatable example of humour is found in 2 Kings 6:8-23. Elisha helps the king of Israel to capture some Aramean soldiers who have been raiding Israel recently. Elijah temporarily blinds them[88] and says-

- 2 Kings 6:19 ... *'This is not the road and this is not the city[89]. Follow me, and I will lead you to the man you are looking for.'* NIV

And so, we enjoy the trickery and just how close Elijah came to lying. Then he leads them to the capital city, where the *king of Israel* just wants to *kill them* all-

- 2 Kings 6:21 *When the king of Israel saw them, he asked Elisha, 'Shall I kill them, my father? Shall I kill them?'* NIV

We laugh at him for being so out of tune with the prevailing mood of mercy. And Elisha insists on overcoming *evil with good* as both Paul and Proverbs tell us[90]-

- Romans 12:21 *Do not be overcome by evil, but overcome evil with good.* NIV

The Arameans meet Elisha, just as he jokingly promised them in verse 21, they go home, and the Aramean raiding parties stop (6:23). This gentle use of humour shows both God's superior power and his generous mercy. It lets even the Arameans know that there is a God in Israel and that his servant is Elisha — all very Christlike. If the king had just killed them, no-one would have gone back to Aram to tell the story (6:22). People need to know about our God, his mercy, and his messenger.

3.6 I and II Chronicles

The book of Chronicles contains much of the material in 2 Samuel and in 1 and 2 Kings, but focuses more on the southern kingdom of Judah. It shows how, not only the Northern kingdom of Samaria (or Israel) deserved to go into exile, but so did the

---

87 A type is a biblical picture of something else, usually of Jesus. See 2 Kings 4:42-44 for example. For more, see *The Transforming Power of God*, John D. Legg, EP, 2008.
88 As you do.
89 "These aren't the droids you're looking for." — Obi-Wan Kenobi in Star Wars Episode IV 'A New Hope'_{TM.} Note that this would still be humorous without the unwitting Star Wars_{TM} allusion.
90 Proverbs 25:21,22

southern kingdom, including those in Jerusalem. None of this sounds like humorous material, nor do the long catalogues of names and tribes in 1 Chronicles 1 to 9.

Indeed, the humour in Chronicles seems to be mainly bad humour. In 1 Chronicles 20:6-7, a giant with six digits on each limb taunted Israel, so David's brother killed him. Taunting the LORD's anointed and his people is simply not funny, Philistine.

In 2 Chronicles 30:6ff, Hezekiah, who is only actually king over the southern kingdom, tries to evangelise the northern kingdom-

- 2 Chronicles 30:10 *The couriers went from town to town in Ephraim and Manasseh, as far as Zebulun, but people scorned and ridiculed them. ¹¹ Nevertheless, some from Asher, Manasseh and Zebulun humbled themselves and went to Jerusalem.* NIV

Hezekiah has limited success, but his couriers are mainly greeted with what the northern kingdom thought was humour, *scorn and ridicule*. However, while they were still laughing, God was heeding Hezekiah's prayers and blessing the people in the southern kingdom-

- 2 Chronicles 30:26 *There was great joy in Jerusalem, for since the days of Solomon son of David king of Israel there had been nothing like this in Jerusalem. ²⁷ The priests and the Levites stood to bless the people, and God heard them, for their prayer reached heaven, his holy dwelling-place.* NIV

Here was revival! But many in the northern kingdom just thought it funny. Not good humour at all. How we need God's blessing in the form of revival in the UK[91]. It is a serious need, not something to be despised.

But, eventually, even the southern kingdom joins in the joking-

- 2 Chronicles 36:16 *But they mocked God's messengers, despised his words and scoffed at his prophets until the wrath of the LORD was aroused against his people and there was no remedy.* NIV

There was no remedy for such persistently sinful humour. No doubt the perpetrators thought it funny, but God did not, and sent them into exile in Babylon, from where most never returned. How we need God to have mercy on the Western world before it is too late and *'there is no remedy'* (36:16).

---

91 And probably where you live, too, dear reader.

****

There is a smidgen of humour in 2 Chronicles 18. The kings of the northern and southern kingdoms trade opinions of the *prophet Micaiah-*

- 2 Chronicles 18:7 *The king of Israel answered Jehoshaphat, 'There is still one prophet through whom we can enquire of the LORD, but I hate him because he never prophesies anything good about me, but always bad. He is Micaiah son of Imlah.'* NIV

That is mildly amusing and shows how we, as humans, only really want to hear what our itching ears have already decided[92]. This use of humour disarms us and helps us to recognise ourselves in the *king of Israel's* bitter statement. Much humour is to do with recognising ourselves, and the Bible makes good use of such humour[93].

The humour continues with an apparent lie-

- 2 Chronicles 18:14 *When he* [the prophet] *arrived, the king asked him, 'Micaiah, shall we go to war against Ramoth Gilead, or shall I not?'*

  'Attack and be victorious,' he answered, 'for they will be given into your hand.'

  [15] *The king said to him, 'How many times must I make you swear to tell me nothing but the truth in the name of the LORD?'* NIV

And it would have been an actual lie, except that *Micaiah* was using humour to expose the *king's* distaste for truth. This is an enlightening example of how we could easily mistake the meaning of scripture if we failed to spot the humour being employed. Here it is ironic trickery, perhaps even teasing.

****

Then there is *King Jehoram's* epitaph-

- 2 Chronicles 21:20 *Jehoram was thirty-two years old when he became king, and he reigned in Jerusalem for eight years. He passed away, to no one's regret, and was buried in the City of David, but not in the tombs of the kings.* NIV

Jehoram had despised the word of the LORD, so he is given this double epitaph, the first part wry and insulting, *'to no-one's regret'*, the second, a summary judgement — he was not *buried* like a proper *king*. This is all rather sarcastic, and fits in well with how Elijah had cursed him previously-

---

92 2 Timothy 4:3
93 Perhaps especially in Proverbs.

- 2 Chronicles 21:15 *You yourself will be very ill with a lingering disease of the bowels, until the disease causes your bowels to come out.* NIV

Those who suffer from any intestinal complaint should absolutely not take this personally. But in *Jehoram's* case, it is recorded in 2 Chronicles in a vulgar and even lavatorial way, to teach a very strong lesson about what a bad *king* looks like, perhaps even what one smells like.[94]

How can we avoid becoming the laughing-stock of scripture?
By never laughing at God's word.

3.7 Ezra

Ezra and Nehemiah both come after the Babylonian exile, but are still in its shadow. Like Chronicles, they are very sober books.

But there is some God-centred teaching that is delivered humorously in Ezra. *Cyrus* thinks he is king (1:2), but both he and, later, Darius (6:22), and finally Artaxerxes (7:27) are firmly under control of the King of Kings, as follows-

- Ezra 1:1 *In the first year of Cyrus king of Persia, in order to fulfil the word of the Lord spoken by Jeremiah, the Lord moved the heart of Cyrus king of Persia …* NIV

- Ezra 6:22 *...the Lord had filled them with joy by changing the attitude of the king of Assyria so that he assisted them in the work on the house of God, …* NIV

- Ezra 7:27 *Praise be to the Lord, the God of our ancestors, who has put it into the king's heart to bring honour to the house of the Lord ...* NIV

The humour is understated[95], but it is very noticeable that whereas *Cyrus* only vaguely provides funding for the temple work, and at everyone else's expense (1:4; 6:8), like a typical politician who just wants the pro-*Cyrus* newspaper headline, Artaxerxes puts his money where his mouth is, and provides hard cash from the royal treasuries (7:15).

Then, in chapter 8, Ezra himself wryly remarks-

- Ezra 8:22 *I was ashamed to ask the king for soldiers and horsemen to protect us from enemies on the road, because we had told the king, 'The gracious hand of our God is on everyone who looks to him...* NIV

---

94 See also 2 Chronicles 21:14 and note that it was those around Jehoram who suffered olfactorily!
95 Litotes or Meiosis

Ezra's self-deprecating humour here challenges us too. Do we, on one hand, say how great *our God* is but, on the other, struggle to trust him ourselves? Again, it is the really important spiritual challenge that disarms us, using humour, and sticks in our memories through causing us to recognise ourselves as the butt of the joke.

3.8 Nehemiah

Nehemiah exhibits anguish through his book. Nine times, he asks God to remember him favourably or to remember his enemies unfavourably (1:8; 4:14; 5:19; 6:14; 9:17; 13:14,22,29,31). His cries to God of, *'Remember me',* become more and more frequent when he comes back from Babylon in chapter 13 only to find that everything had gone wrong while he was away: The temple was being misused, foreigners were taking over (again), the Levites had not been paid, the Sabbath broken and, perhaps worst of all, God's people had started marrying the local pagans!

Nehemiah throws a tantrum and summarises the ridiculous situation-

- Nehemiah 13:24 *Half of their children spoke the language of Ashdod or the language of one of the other peoples, and did not know how to speak the language of Judah.* NIV

And then-

- Nehemiah 13:25 *I rebuked them and called curses down on them. I beat some of the men and pulled out their hair.* NIV

We cringe at the seriousness of the situation and grit our teeth at Nehemiah's perseverance, but didn't you also find it hard to suppress a smile when he started *pulling* people's *hair out*? And laugh we should, but also remember the occasion very clearly. The seriousness and stupidity of these *Judahites* who married the local pagans cannot be overstated. We would never do anything like that, would we?[96]

3.9 Esther

The book of Esther opens with a stratospheric description of the King *Xerxes'*[97] greatness-

- Esther 1:1 *This is what happened during the time of Xerxes, the Xerxes who ruled over 127 provinces stretching from India to Cush…* NIV

Not only was he a big emperor, but his parties were also big-

---

96 I Corinthians 7:39
97 He is normally known by this name, *Xerxes,* being a transliteration of his name in Greek. The Hebrew form is Ahasuerus.

- Esther 1:4 *For a full 180 days he displayed the vast wealth of his kingdom and the splendour and glory of his majesty. ⁵ When these days were over, the king gave a banquet, lasting seven days, in the enclosed garden of the king's palace, for all the people from the least to the greatest who were in the citadel of Susa. ⁶ The garden had hangings of white and blue linen, fastened with cords of white linen and purple material to silver rings on marble pillars. There were couches of gold and silver on a mosaic pavement of porphyry, marble, mother-of-pearl and other costly stones. ⁷ Wine was served in goblets of gold, each one different from the other, and the royal wine was abundant, in keeping with the king's liberality. ⁸ By the king's command each guest was allowed to drink without restriction, for the king instructed all the wine stewards to serve each man what he wished.* NIV

In fact, everything about him was larger than life, until his trophy wife…-

- Esther 1:11 … *Queen Vashti, wearing her royal crown, in order to display her beauty to the people and nobles, for she was lovely to look at,* … NIV

… refused to take to the catwalk. She was a feminist. She had 'burned her bra'. No way was she going to be paraded (half?) naked in front of Xerxes' drunken party-goers! But the lesson of the chapter is nothing to do with feminism or women's suffrage.

The humour is at *King Xerxes'* expense: The *king* in control of *127 provinces* cannot even control his wife. Furthermore, he cannot decide what to do with her without the aid of his royal eunuchs (1:13-15). But eventually an official decision is made, and the empirical 'internet' bursts into life-

- Esther 1:22 *He sent dispatches to all parts of the kingdom, to each province in its own script and to each people in their own language, proclaiming that every man should be ruler over his own household, using his native tongue.* NIV

Radical stuff. In fact, it is difficult to point out the humour without simply copying and pasting the whole chapter, because the writing is inherently funny from beginning to end!

After much marinating in royal perfume[98], Esther becomes queen, but is immediately under the threat of genocide together with the rest of the Jews

---

98   Esther 2:12

because of the evil *Haman*. Jewish people know how to enjoy Esther. The reading of Esther is such a central part of the feast of Purim, that Jews traditionally hiss, boo, and use the equivalent of football rattles, during the reading, in order to annihilate *Haman's* very name!

We laugh at the evil *Haman* when the very man he is trying to take revenge on, Esther's uncle *Mordecai*, gets *honoured*-

- Esther 6:6 *When Haman entered, the king asked him, 'What should be done for the man the king delights to honour?'*

  Now Haman thought to himself, 'Who is there that the king would rather honour than me?' [7] *So he answered the king, 'For the man the king delights to honour,* [8] *let them bring a royal robe the king has worn and a horse the king has ridden, one with a royal crest placed on its head.* [9] *Then let the robe and horse be entrusted to one of the king's most noble princes. Let them robe the man the king delights to honour, and lead him on the horse through the city streets, proclaiming before him, "This is what is done for the man the king delights to honour!"'*

  [10] *'Go at once,' the king commanded Haman. 'Get the robe and the horse and do just as you have suggested for Mordecai the Jew*[99]*...* NIV

And we laugh when *Haman's* plot to kill all the *Jews* including the queen is finally revealed, with the result that *Haman* is hanged on his own gallows or, more likely, impaled on his own pole (7:9,10), the one he had specially erected for *Mordecai*!

But why are we laughing at such grim and gory history? The answer has to be that this is how scripture portrays God's attitude to his enemies (Psalm 2), and to the enemies of his precious people: Humour.

And the big joke in the book of Esther is that this God, who provides for and protects his people, is not even mentioned or alluded to once in the whole book!

Here, now, so often, he is in the *'still small voice of calm'*[100] (a *gentle whisper'* in 1 Kings 19:12). So often, he *'plants his footsteps in the sea'*[101] (Psalm 77:19) so that they cannot be seen, except by faith. We must trust and persevere, especially when we cannot see our God, except by trusting him, except through his promises, except

---

99 Again, there is a danger here of simply quoting the whole chapter.
100 The famous hymn, *Dear Lord and Father*, is pure drivel IMO. The tune, *Repton* by Hubert Parry, is fabulous, but only serves to disguise the very weak theology.
101 In complete contrast with the above, William Cowper's hymn, *God moves in a Mysterious Way*, is magnificent, theological, but could do with a better tune than *Dundee* IMO.

in our Bibles. How we must make good use of the *'ordinary means of grace'* before life gets tough.[102]

4. Humour In The Wisdom Books

The wisdom books teach us to live wisely in life's various situations.

4.1 Job

Job is about how to suffer wisely, but that does not mean that there is no room for humour, especially biblical humour.

One big area of suffering for Job is that he himself has become the butt of the joke-

- Job 12:4 *'I have become a laughing-stock to my friends,*
  though I called on God and he answered –
  a mere laughing-stock, though righteous and blameless![103]

Job protests his innocence, but his friends promise that he will only get to be the one who is doing the *laughing* if and when he repents-

- Job 5:22 *You will laugh at destruction and famine, ...*

But the serious humour only arrives when God starts to speak. At first, he seems scathing about Job's pitiful attempts to understand divine ways-

- Job 38:2 *'Who is this that obscures my plans*
  with words without knowledge?' NIV

Then, the LORD summons up several images of things that Job cannot hope to understand, some of which are quite humorous-

- Job 38:31 *'Can you bind the chains* [or beauty] *of the Pleiades*[104]*?*
  Can you loosen Orion's belt?

---

102 Westminster Shorter Catechism 1646/7 *Q.88. What are the outward and ordinary means whereby Christ communicates to us the benefits of redemption? A. The outward and ordinary means whereby Christ communicates to us the benefits of redemption, are his ordinances, especially the word, sacraments, and prayer; all which are made effectual to the elect for salvation.*

103 See also 17:2; 19:18; 21:3; 30:1-9.

104 A constellation, the *'Seven Sisters'*.

Figure 9: The constellation of Orion, with belt clearly visible. Wiki media commons, Creative Commons License(sic) 3.0

Shut your eyes and try to imagine the comical image of Job helping *Orion* with his *belt* (especially as Orion is a constellation, not a Greek giant!)

Then there is the *behemoth*-

- Job 40:24 *Can anyone capture it by the eyes,
  or trap it and pierce its nose?* NIV

Can anyone treat this monster like a domestic animal?

Even more sarcastically, how about the *Leviathan*?-

- Job 40:1 *'Can you pull in Leviathan with a fish-hook
  or tie down its tongue with a rope?
  ² Can you put a cord through its nose
  or pierce its jaw with a hook?
  ³ Will it keep begging you for mercy?
  Will it speak to you with gentle words?'* NIV

What a ridiculous idea. The humour gently teaches Job just how far off he is from even beginning to understand God's ways.

And the big joke in the book? Job never seems to find out the cause of all his suffering![105] And nor may we; we have to keep trusting and obeying God, whether we understand or not, as the key verse in Job explains-

- Job 28:28 *'And he said to the human race,*
  'The fear of the Lord — that is wisdom,
  and to shun evil is understanding.' NIV

These late chapters in Job (28 to 42) are humorous, humbling, memorable and profound. They must be allowed to tame our frustration during times of suffering.

4.2 Psalms

The five books of psalms are about how to worship wisely, where the word 'worship' embraces the whole of life and the whole of creation-

- Psalm 150:6 *Let everything that has breath praise the LORD.* NIV

Although Psalms is not narrative, i.e. not a story, it is large and contains plenty of humour. The psalms cover the full range of human experience, particularly focussing on the experiences of the godly at the hands of the wicked, and at the tongues of the wicked-

- Psalm 42:10 *My bones suffer mortal agony*
  as my foes taunt me,
  saying to me all day long,
  'Where is your God?' NIV

See also 22:7;35:16;44:16; 55:12; 69:9,12; 73:8; 74:10,18,22; 80:6; 89:50,51; 102:8; 119:42,51; 123:4. In all these psalms, the writer endures mockery, insult, taunting, scoffing and ridicule, all of which seem humorous to the wicked at the time. But, in the long term, who will have the last laugh? It will be *the LORD*: He is already *laughing* at his enemies-

- Psalm 37:13 *'but the Lord laughs at the wicked,*
  for he knows their day is coming' NIV

And, one day, his persecuted people will *laugh* too-

- Psalm 126:1 *When the LORD restored the fortunes of Zion,*
  we were like those who dreamed.
  ² Our mouths were filled with laughter,
  our tongues with songs of joy.

---

105 Unless, perhaps he is its author, however, even then he only discovered why it all happened afterwards.

This is a new kind of *laughter*, a kind that goes beyond the *scoffing* in Psalm 2:4, a flavour of humour that we have not really noticed before[106]. It is the kind of laughter that happens when *the LORD* turns our misery into *joy*. Is it perhaps a triumphal kind of humour?

Fools are also addressed in the Psalms, although the detailed treatment of human folly is reserved for the book of Proverbs. In Psalm 53-

- Psalm 53:1 *The fool says in his heart, 'There is no God'* NIV

But later-

- Psalm 53:5 *...there they are, overwhelmed with dread,*
  where there was nothing to dread. NIV

The psalm invites the believer to smile on all those occasions when atheists run scared, but there is nothing to run from! Think of the myriad films about meteors colliding with earth, the extinction of humanity, how we simply must populate Mars to reduce the risk of humans dying out! Proverbs agrees-

- Proverbs 28:1 *The wicked flee though no-one is pursuing,*
  but the righteous are as bold as a lion.

****

Figure 10: Psalm 23:5
'You prepare a table before me'
Public Domain, https://www.stock-free.org

---

106 But do refer back to the section on Deuteronomy, where *triumph* is mentioned.

Psalm 23 is so often, and rightly, used at funerals, that we might not look there first for humour. Even though David is walking *through the darkest valley* (23:4), *he fears no evil*. He knows that he is immortal[107] until the day that *the LORD,* his *shepherd,* has ordained to take him to be with himself.

And then, David has this delightful vision of himself sitting at a picnic *table* laden with food, and enjoying a leisurely meal while his *enemies* look on, somehow, unable to attack!

- *Psalm 23:5 You prepare a table before me*
    in the presence of my enemies. NIV

The LORD holds David's life in his hands, and David knows that he is eternally safe *in the house of the LORD* (23:6). The humorous image is surprising, because of the juxtapositioning of enemies and a meal *table,* but expresses a very sober faith in God.

****

Previously, we noticed Elisha, a clear type of Christ, being taunted[108], but the Messiah himself is explicitly mocked in Psalm 22[109]-

- Psalm 22:7 *All who see me mock me;*
    they hurl insults, shaking their heads.
    [8] *'He trusts in the LORD,' they say,*
    'let the LORD rescue him. NIV

The Messiah is *mocked* and, thereby, our only means of salvation is *insulted*. It was impossible for *the LORD* to *rescue* the Messiah. If God had *rescued* him, he could not have rescued the ones for whom the Messiah was dying. Humour of the *mocking* and *insulting* kinds are even bound up with the cross, and humour finds itself near to the very heart of the gospel: Jesus suffering and dying.

---

107 As Henry Martyn said - Missionary – 1781 (Cornwall) – 1812 (Tokat, Ottoman Empire)

108 2 Kings 2

109 See also Psalm 42:10. Matthew 27:39ff and Mark 15:29-32, which confirm Psalm 22 as messianic.

Figure 11: The Judgement of Solomon by Peter Paul Rubens (1577-1640), Public Domain

4.3 Proverbs

Proverbs is about how to live wisely. Contrary to what we might at first assume, the wise engage in plenty of humour. Indeed, Proverbs deals in different categories of people, and is never politically correct about putting people in boxes, or of otherwise 'giving a dog a bad name'. Refreshing.

The main categories are the *wise* and the *foolish*, but these split down into more categories according to the Hebrew words that are carefully selected by the writers. Bruce Waltke in his commentary[110] finds the following theological categories[111]: the *wise*, the *righteous*, the *wicked*, the *unrighteous*, the *mocker*, the *perverse*, the *evildoer*, the *gullible* or *simple*, the *fool* (represented by two Hebrew words), the *sluggard*, the *adulteress* or *adulterous*, the *wayward wife*, and the *unfaithful*. The *poor*, the *rich*, the *gossip*, *drunkard* and *glutton* must also be added to the list of categories[112], when considering humour in Proverbs.

---

110 The Book of Proverbs, Eerdmans, 2004, 2 volumes
111 And others. It is a very large, two volume, commentary.
112 And there are many others.

The main categories to which humour is mainly applied seem to be-

- The *sluggard* (26:13-19)

- The *drunkard* (23:29-35)

- The *adulteress* or *adulterous* (6:20-7:27)

- The *gossip* or joker

It is noticeable that humour is not generally used to describe the *wise* (*the righteous*), nor usually even those named explicitly as *fools* (*the unrighteous*). Perhaps the most immediately accessible and evocative humour in Proverbs is reserved for the *sluggard-*

- Proverbs 6:6 *Go to the ant, you sluggard; consider its ways and be wise!* NIV

- Proverbs 10:26 *As vinegar to the teeth and smoke to the eyes, so are sluggards to those who send them.* NIV

- Proverbs 19:24 *A sluggard buries his hand in the dish; he will not even bring it back to his mouth!* NIV

- Proverbs 22:13 *The sluggard says, 'There's a lion outside! I'll be killed in the public square!'* NIV

- Proverbs 26:14 *As a door turns on its hinges, so a sluggard turns on his bed.* NIV

The hope of the writer of Proverbs is that we will recognise ourselves through its humour, be disarmed, and thereby enabled to repent.

Proverbs has a whole 'saying' devoted to the *drunkard-*

- Proverbs 23:33 *Your eyes will see strange sights, and your mind will imagine confusing things.*
  [34] You will be like one sleeping on the high seas, lying on top of the rigging.
  [35] 'They hit me,' you will say, 'but I'm not hurt! They beat me, but I don't feel it! When will I wake up so I can find another drink?' NIV

It is tragic, but at the same time very funny. My wife's comment was that this passage makes you feel sea-sick just by reading it! Once again the writer hopes that we will recognise ourselves in the humorous description, and repent.

Chapters 5, 6 and 7 have a lot to say about the *adulterous*, and in particular, the *adulteress*. These chapters are thick with sarcasm, even pathos, and shock-

- Proverbs 6:26 *For a prostitute can be had for a loaf of bread*[113],
    but another man's wife preys on your very life.
    27 Can a man scoop fire into his lap
    without his clothes being burned?
    28 Can a man walk on hot coals
    without his feet being scorched?
    29 So is he who sleeps with another man's wife;
    no one who touches her will go unpunished. NIV

The adulteress is pictured as a huntress, then *fire* and *hot coals*! Proverbs jeers at the potential adulterer, "How could you be that stupid?", thus motivating him towards sexual morality by its vivid humour.

Chapter 7 is similarly evocative-

- Proverbs 7:26 *Many are the victims she has brought down;*
    her slain are a mighty throng.
    27 Her house is a highway to the grave,
    leading down to the chambers of death. NIV

Both male and female Christians need to meditate on such wisdom; we need to allow the humour to soak into our consciences so that when temptation arises we are defended by wisdom, by highly memorable, humorous, treasures of wisdom.

****

Proverbs also has warning about the wrong use of humour-

- Proverbs 10:23 *Doing wrong is like a joke to a fool,*
    but wisdom is pleasure to a man of understanding. NIV

Humour should never be used as camouflage for wrong-doing.

Careless joking can have dire consequences-

- Proverbs 26:18 *Like a maniac shooting flaming arrows of death*
    19 is one who deceives their neighbour and says, 'I was only joking!' NIV

****

---

113 The 1984 NIV and others have '*reduces you to a loaf of bread*' (or similar), which is sadly humorous. Waltke discusses the difficulty of translating this verse on page 354 of his commentary on Proverbs. In any case the second line of the verse is vivid humour.

And many, proverbs are simply laugh-out-loud funny, pointed and memorable-

- Proverbs 11:22 says, *Like a gold ring in a pig's snout
  is a beautiful woman who shows no discretion.* NIV

- Proverbs 21:19 *Better to live on a corner of the roof
  than share a house with a quarrelsome wife.* NIV

- Proverbs 27:14 *If a man loudly blesses his neighbour early in the
  morning,
  it will be taken as a curse.* NIV

And then we are reminded that humour is not a reliable solution to life's problems-

- Proverbs 14:13 *Even in laughter the heart may ache,
  and rejoicing may end in grief.* NIV

Nor is money[114]-

- Proverbs 23:5 *Cast but a glance at riches, and they are gone,
  for they will surely sprout wings and fly off to the sky like an eagle.* NIV

These examples all contain very memorable wisdom, and are quite often disturbing. The humour often has quite an 'edge' to it, and never worries about offending anyone. Very little updating to the 21st Century is required in order to apply such wisdom to ourselves.

There is a sharp dividing line between the *wise* and the *foolish*, the *righteous* and the *evil*. The constant question (from the point of view of humour, at least) is whether we want to be in heaven laughing for ever, or in Sheol where there will never be any laughter.

4.4 Ecclesiastes

Attempts to impose a structure on the book of Ecclesiastes have failed to reach any kind of consensus, however Barry Webb[115] (in my opinion) gives us a useful key with which to decode Ecclesiastes' peculiar kind of wisdom. He asserts that Ecclesiastes is composed of '*observations*' and '*instructions*'. These alternate in a non-rigid manner throughout the book, so-

---

114 Cf. *Money* in Ecclesiastes 10:19
115 *Five Festal Garments*, IVP, 2000, p87

> 1:3 - 4:16 is *observation*.
>
> 5:1 - 9 is *instruction*.
>
> 5:10 - 6:9 is *observation*.
>
> 6:10 - 7:22 is *instruction*.
>
> 7:23 - 29 is *observation*.
>
> 8:1 - 8 is *instruction*.
>
> 8:9 - 9:12 is *observation*.
>
> 9:13 - 12:7 is *instruction*.
>
> 12:8 is a brief *observation*.[116]
>
> 12:9 - 14 is *instruction*.

I, myself, would prefer a more detailed division between the *observational* passages and the *instructional* ones, but I believe his approach is essentially correct. The *instructional* passages contain wisdom that has been revealed to Solomon, and is now issued to the reader as mainly commands, for example-

- Ecclesiastes 5:1 *Guard your steps when you go to the house of God. Go near to listen rather than to offer the sacrifice of fools, who do not know that they do wrong.* NIV

The *instructional* passages are marked primarily by references to *God*.

The *observational* passages also contain wisdom, but of a different kind. It is the wisdom that Solomon[117] has gained through all his 'life experiments'-

- Ecclesiastes 1:12 *I, the Teacher, was king over Israel in Jerusalem. [13] I applied my mind to study and to explore by wisdom all that is done under the heavens.* NIV

These observational wisdom sections are marked by key phrases such as '*under the heavens*', '*under the sun*' and the single word refrain '*Meaningless*'[118].

---

116 This deviates slightly from Barry Webb's proposed structure.

117 Solomon is called 'The Teacher'.

118 The word *meaningless* in Ecclesiastes means 'hard to understand', 'spoiled by sin/the Fall/the curse', seemingly pointless', 'merely temporary', — a whole range of complex ideas! See Barry Webb for more on this subject.

What then of humour in Ecclesiastes? The humour is definitely, but perhaps not exclusively, concentrated within the *observational* sections, for example-

- Ecclesiastes 1:11 *No one remembers the former generations, …*

This is a kind of sad hyperbole, filled with pathos, but not absolutely, always, true; we do remember Solomon, for example. But this (1:11) is Solomon's observation of what tends to happen after normal people die. Here is Solomon's observation about humour itself-

- Ecclesiastes 2:2 *"Laughter," I said, "is madness.*
  And what does pleasure accomplish?" NIV

Here is a key *observation* in Ecclesiastes, but expressed using a ridiculous idea-

- 2:26c *This too is meaningless, a chasing after the wind.* NIV

In contrast, when Solomon starts to relate some revealed, *instructional*, wisdom, he issues crisp commands, with no hint of humour-

- Ecclesiastes 5:4 *When you make a vow to God, do not delay fulfilling it.*

However, when he reveals some *observational* wisdom, the rules are less tight, so there is room for a short, funny, story-

- 4:13 *Better a poor but wise youth than an old but foolish king who no longer knows how to heed a warning. [14] The youth may have come from prison to the kingship, or he may have been born in poverty within his kingdom. [15] I saw that all who lived and walked under the sun followed the youth, the king's successor. [16] There was no end to all the people who were before them. But those who came later were not pleased with the successor. This too is meaningless, a chasing after the wind.* NIV

The book's ending is purely *instructional* wisdom, and deadly serious, with no room for humour-

- Ecclesiastes 12:1 *Remember your Creator in the days of your youth, …*

And-

- Ecclesiastes 12:14 *For God will bring every deed into judgement,*
  including every hidden thing,
  whether it is good or evil. NIV

If it is true that the humour is concentrated in the *observational* wisdom sections, then, if we use Webb's suggested structure (above), the following scathing *observation* would seem to find itself awkwardly right in the middle of an *instructional* section-

- Ecclesiastes 7:6 *Like the crackling of thorns under the pot,*
    so is the laughter of fools. NIV

But if, as I personally suspect, the whole of the section running from 6:3 to 7:12 is actually composed of *observational* wisdom, then the problem of 7:6 goes away. In this way, perhaps we can assign each section to the categories of either *observation* or *instruction* partly by using the criterion that only *observational* sections contain humour[119]?

Whatever we decide about the structure of Ecclesiastes, it certainly makes good use of humour-

- Ecclesiastes 7:21 *Do not pay attention to every word people say,*
    or you may hear your servant cursing you... NIV

And-

- Ecclesiastes 7:28 *...while I was still searching but not finding,*
    I found one upright man among a thousand,
        but not one upright woman among them all. NIV

How did Solomon discover this sexist-sounding piece of wisdom? Well it is not really sexist; it merely reflects Solomon's own discovery, having had 700 wives![120] We can definitely say that Solomon was a wiser man at the end of the process than at the beginning!

Furthermore, if we should say that Solomon was a nasty sexist, and told a blatant lie, when he implied that *women* are never *upright*, it would be because we had failed to notice that-

a) 7:28 is in an *observational* section of wisdom that reflects Solomon's own experience, and

b) it is probably hyperbole, a piece of humour, overstated in order to make a point that women are likely to relate to a powerful man (i.e. the king) in a dishonest way, and that the men are hardly any better.[121]

****

---

119 However, in the case of a book like Ecclesiastes, I would hesitate to be absolutely black and white about such a criterion.

120 1 Kings 11:3, and 300 concubines!

121 Also, the alternation from 'one upright' to 'not one upright' probably achieved the balance required by the inherent parallelism in Hebrew poetry.

Not only does Ecclesiastes use humour to impart its wisdom, but it also addresses the subject of humour itself-

- Ecclesiastes 2:2 *'Laughter,' I said, 'is madness.*
  And what does pleasure accomplish?' NIV

- Ecclesiastes 3:4 [*There is*] *...a time to weep and a time to laugh*

- Ecclesiastes 10:19 *A feast is made for laughter, and wine makes life merry,*
  but money is the answer for everything. NIV

The sober conclusion tells us that even our use of humour must be wise, for it too will one day be judged by God-

- Ecclesiastes 12:14 *For God will bring every deed into judgement,*
  including every hidden thing[122],
  whether it is good or evil. NIV

Have we Christians used humour wisely and in the kinds of ways that the Bible does? Or have we used it badly, in a way that is unnecessarily scathing, despising or demeaning? Have we used it as a cover for some sin? Or, have we used it to lift the mood, share our joy, or to make some teaching punchy and memorable? Ecclesiastes makes me want to review all my footnotes and sermon notes, and check them for side-swipes, unkindnesses, or unnecessary derogatory humour.

4.5 The Song of Songs (or of Solomon)

The Song of Solomon seems devoid of humour. Is the subject of how to love, wisely, just too sensitive for humour? I think so.

There is plenty of emotion, even passion, in the book, but none of it seems involve humour. Some have read some 'nudge-nudge, wink-wink', humour into it, but they have failed to see that any sexual references are certainly not double entendres; rather they are exactly what they seem to be, and are all set in the context of a marriage.

---

122 Matthew 12:36 *"But I tell you that everyone will have to give account on the day of judgement for every empty word they have spoken."*

5. Humour in the Major Prophets

5.1 Isaiah

In 701BC, *Hezekiah* was a godly and experienced king, having been on the throne of Judah for fourteen years. When the Assyrian king, *Sennacherib*, comes to attack Jerusalem, having had great success with attacking everyone else in the area, he says to the people of Jerusalem in their own language-

- Isaiah 36:4 *"...on what are you basing this confidence of yours? [5] You say you have counsel and might for war — but you speak only empty words. On whom are you depending, that you rebel against me? [6] Look, I know you are depending on Egypt, that splintered reed of a staff, which pierces the hand of anyone who leans on it! Such is Pharaoh king of Egypt to all who depend on him."* NIV

The attacker employs sarcasm to dismiss any thought of help from *Egypt*. Then, because mere sarcasm is apparently not offensive enough, he continues-

- Isaiah 36:7 *"But if you say to me, 'We are depending on the LORD our God'– isn't he the one whose high places and altars Hezekiah removed, saying to Judah and Jerusalem, 'You must worship before this altar'?"* NIV

Leaving aside the obvious mistake about *Hezekiah removing the LORD's altars*, this has now become a straightforward insult to *God,* and a contradiction of the very gospel itself, i.e. *'depending on the LORD'.*

So, *Hezekiah* prays, and the prophet Isaiah replies to *Sennacherib* with *mockery* and derision-

- Isaiah 37:22 *'Virgin Daughter Zion[123]*
    despises and mocks you.
  Daughter Jerusalem
    tosses her head as you flee.
  [23] Who is it you have ridiculed and blasphemed?
    Against whom have you raised your voice
  and lifted your eyes in pride?
    Against the Holy One of Israel[124]! NIV

---

123 It is generally thought nowadays that the *virgin daughter* is *Zion,* not just the women who live in *Zion.* See Barry Webb's IVP commentary on Isaiah.

124 Isaiah's favourite ways of referring to God

The salvoes of vitriolic humour go back and forth, but he who laughs last laughs longest-

- Isaiah 37:36 *Then the angel of the* LORD *went out and put to death a 185,000 in the Assyrian camp.* NIV

And, around 20 years later-

- Isaiah 37:38 *One day, while he* [Sennacherib] *was worshipping in the temple of his god Nisrok, his sons Adrammelek and Sharezer killed him with the sword...*

There are three punch lines here:

1. *Sennacherib's* attack is entirely defeated by the *angel of the LORD.*

2. *Sennacherib* is assassinated by *his sons.* Yes, *the LORD* did that too.

3. *Sennacherib* gets assassinated in the very temple of *his god* who, it is implied, completely failed to protect him, unlike *the LORD* who protected *Hezekiah.*

We may just read that as blood-thirsty, but it is not; it is biblical humour, laughing at those who would dare to insult the living God. Humour is being employed to challenge every reader in a biblically crude and humorous way, as if saying, 'Whose side are you on?' The answer is very serious. This kind of crude discrimination does not jive well with the western liberalised air that we breathe. But the humour in the passage, cuts through all such world views, readjusts our outlook, makes us more biblical in the way we think, simplifies our broken logic, and galvanises our faith in *the Holy One of Israel.*

****

It is obvious that Hezekiah has been paying close attention to Isaiah's ministry. So when he prays, he says that the *Assyrians* ...-

- Isaiah 37:19 ... *have thrown the other nations' gods into the fire and destroyed them, for they were not gods but only wood and stone, fashioned by human hands.*

Perhaps *King Hezekiah* even laughed when he read the long and highly amusing passage in Isaiah 44, all of it pouring scorn on *idols* and those who worship them. It is a long but self-explanatory passage. The gist of it is that *idols* are worthless; they cannot foretell the future, they are made by blacksmiths and carpenters; one half of a piece of wood gets used as firewood, the other gets made into an *idol* and *worshipped*!-

- Isaiah 44:17 *From the rest he makes a god, his idol;*
    he bows down to it and worships.
  He prays to it and says,
    'Save me! You are my god!' NIV

Just read Isaiah 44:6-22; it is laugh-out-loud humour and, once again, is employed in the service of God, and on a topic of great gravity: Idolatry.

5.2 Jeremiah

Apart from the occasional word-play (1:11: *almond tree*, שָׁקֵד, *shaqed*, and 1:12 *watching*, שֹׁקֵד, *shoqed*), the humour in Jeremiah is mainly of the gloomy sort. His sixth and longest 'confession' or 'complaint' in 20:7-18 contains what seems to be a crisis of faith. He accuses *the LORD* of deceiving him by conning him into being a prophet (as recorded in 1:4-8)-

- Jeremiah 20:7cd *I am ridiculed all day long;*
    everyone mocks me ...

- 8cd *So the word of the LORD has brought me*
    insult and reproach all day long.

He has become the butt of the humour, and is clearly finding it hard to bear. We should never assume that humour is a light thing. It is a difficult thing to endure. Elsewhere, he is scoffed at, put down a hole, and taken forcibly off to Egypt where, presumably he dies[125].

But Jeremiah gives as good as he gets. In chapter 10, like Isaiah, he mocks Israel's idols-

- Jeremiah 10;14 *Everyone is senseless and without knowledge;*
    every goldsmith is shamed by his idols.
  The images he makes are a fraud;
    they have no breath in them.
    [15] *They are worthless, the objects of mockery*; NIV

He warns that Jerusalem will be scoffed at (19:8), as will Edom and Babylon (49:17; 50:13). They, and their *idols,* will all be destroyed. We really need to take biblical warnings against idolatry seriously.

---

125 Jeremiah 42:17

We might never be foolish enough to bow down to wooden or metal idols, but the danger of idolatry lurks continuously. John Calvin wrote, '*the human mind is, so to speak, a perpetual forge of idols*'.[126] Our automotive idols can sit in the gutter and drink petrol[127]. Our one-eyed idols sit in the corner of our living rooms[128]. Males' idols are commonly objects — cars, toys, computers; females' idols are commonly relational — children, grandchildren, friendships etc. Social idols include equality, education, the NHS. Idols on which we depend, and put much of our faith in, include pensions, salaries and wealth in general.

Most idols are perfectly good things in themselves, but automatically become idols when we rely on them instead of on God. Even basics, like food[129], can become a cruel idol, although we call it 'comfort eating' nowadays.

Nothing has really changed since Jeremiah's time, so we need to allow the caustic humour in scripture that is used to mock idols and idolaters really to sink into our naturally idolatrous hearts. As Jeremiah said-

- Jeremiah 17:9 *The heart is deceitful above all things*
  and beyond cure.
  Who can understand it? NIV

5.3 Lamentations

Jeremiah's other book, Lamentations, is really another wisdom book. It teaches us how to grieve wisely. Written in response to the destruction of Jerusalem in 586BC, all the humour belongs to the victorious enemy. The enemy laughs at Jerusalem's demise (1:7); passers-by *scoff* (2:16) and employ biting irony and sarcasm-

- Lamentations 2:15 *All who pass your way*
  clap their hands at you;
  they scoff and shake their heads
  at Daughter Jerusalem:
  'Is this the city that was called

---

126 Insitutes Chapter 11 Paragraph 8, in English translation on-line at CCEL:
  http://www.ccel.org/ccel/calvin/institutes.iii.xii.html
127 That is 'gas'.
128 Televisions do not look so 'one-eyed' nowadays, but perhaps that only increases the danger?
129 Colossians 3:5 *Put to death, therefore, whatever belongs to your earthly nature: sexual immorality, impurity, lust, evil desires and greed, which is idolatry.*

the perfection of beauty,
the joy of the whole earth?' NIV

There are even physical actions representing humour, *'clap their hands'*.

And in chapter 3, Jeremiah is once again the laughing-stock (3:14; 3:61) who features in the enemy's *songs-*

- Lamentations 3:63 *Look at them! Sitting or standing, they mock me in their songs.* NIV

There is almost comical injustice here: Jeremiah's prophecies and predictions have all come true (e.g. 38:3), yet he is the one being laughed at!

Referring to events during the first world war, Winston Churchill said, *"No event since the beginning of the Christian era is more likely to strengthen and restore Man's faith in the moral governance of the universe."* [130] Churchill's Christianity was somewhat nominal, but he believed that there would be justice in the end. This will only happen, according to Jeremiah, when the LORD acts to bring justice (Lamentations 3:64), to pay back the enemies of Jerusalem.

When we ourselves experience the injustice of others laughing at us for being Christian, moral, faithful to God, or for putting first the kingdom of God, it is natural to want immediate justice, but often impossible for us to achieve. Furthermore, we are told by Paul to leave room for God's vengeance[131]. When we are on the receiving end of injustice, we need to learn to grieve properly as demonstrated in Lamentations.

5.4 Ezekiel

Ezekiel has all the same taunting and laughter at God's unfaithful people as Jeremiah and Lamentations have (5:15; 22:4,5;36:4,15). But there is also a curious new kind of humour in Ezekiel. Ezekiel is ordered to prophesy to inanimate objects. Being ordered to prophesy itself is a feature of Ezekiel far more than of other books, but prophesying specifically to lifeless things?-

- Ezekiel 6:2 *'Son of man, set your face against the mountains of Israel; prophesy against them…'* NIV

- Ezekiel 20:46 *'Son of man, set your face towards the south; preach against the south and prophesy against the forest of the south land. 47 Say to the southern forest: "Hear the word of the LORD."'*

---

130 Maurice Cowling, *Religion and Public Doctrine in Modern England*, Cambridge University Press, 2001
131 Romans 12:19

- 21:2 *'Son of man, set your face against Jerusalem and preach against the sanctuary.'* NIV

Sometimes, Ezekiel is ordered to prophesy directly against a group of people, e.g. *'shepherds'* (34:2) and sometimes, even when he is ordered to prophesy against an object, it is actually just a way of referring indirectly to a group of people, e.g.-

- Ezekiel 35:2 *'Son of man, set your face against Mount Seir…'* NIV

So, in the above example, *'Mount Seir'* is simply a way of referring to the Edomites who lived there. But commonly, it is geographical features that are personified and prophesied to-

- Ezekiel 36:2 *"'… The ancient heights* [i.e. inanimate mountains] *have become our possession.'"* [3] *Therefore prophesy and say, "This is what the Sovereign LORD says: because they ravaged and crushed you from every side so that you became the possession of the rest of the nations … "'*

And then, even the famous *dry bones* are *prophesied* to as objects, rather than as people-

- Ezekiel 37:4 *Then he said to me, 'Prophesy to these bones and say to them, "Dry bones, hear the word of the LORD!"'* NIV

When reading chapter 37, one has to put out of the mind well-known, funny, song lyrics. But even when the song about *'dem dry bones'* is ignored, there is still something ridiculous about Ezekiel talking to dead *bones*. And *prophesying* to mountains that cannot hear seems even more ridiculous when we remember that Ezekiel was speaking from many hundred of miles away by the River Kebar (1:1). Why would he use this strange device of addressing the inanimate and the distant?

The *dry bones* are addressed in their deadness to highlight God's people's spiritual deadness. Presumably the distant *mountains* are addressed to make the point that the people are in exile and a long way from home. The geographical features of the promised land are prophesied to, because they are now empty of God's cursed[132] and exiled people.

All this seems to be a unique use of personification, together with a type of irony, possibly even sarcasm. Talking *snakes* in Genesis 3 and a talking

---

132 Covenants often have both promises and curses in them. See my Covenants for Evangelicals for more.

donkey in Numbers 22 seem to bode ill. Likewise, personified buildings[133], countryside and *bones* seem to indicate that something is very wrong. Heaven forbid that we should be so out of touch, that God has to address himself to our empty chapels, verdant countryside and beautiful crematoria.

Ezekiel ends, in chapters 40 to 48, with a vision of a holy temple, that was only to be described to the exiles if and when they felt ashamed of their sins (43:10,11). Do we feel genuinely ashamed of our own sins, or are we just sorry that we got found out?

5.5 Daniel

The book of Daniel is full of humour of many kinds, but the practical joke played on King Nebuchadnezzar stands out as particularly stark and memorable. One suspects that we are already meant to be laughing at Nebuchadnezzar at the beginning of Daniel 3; in the previous chapter, he has declared to *Daniel-*

• Daniel 2:47 '*... Surely your God is the God of gods and the Lord of kings...*'

But then, he builds himself an idol 90 feet high, and forces everyone to worship it!

Later, Nebuchadnezzar seems to have forgotten about the true *God* altogether, and we read-

• Daniel 4:29 *Twelve months later, as the king was walking on the roof of the royal palace of Babylon, [30] he said, 'Is not this the great Babylon I have built as the royal residence, by my mighty power and for the glory of my majesty?'*

   [31] Even as the words were on his lips, a voice came from heaven, 'This is what is decreed for you, King Nebuchadnezzar: your royal authority has been taken from you. [32] You will be driven away from people and will live with the wild animals; you will eat grass like the ox. Seven times will pass by for you until you acknowledge that the Most High is sovereign over all kingdoms on earth and gives them to anyone he wishes.' NIV

Now maybe 'practical joke' is not exactly the right way to describe what God does to Nebuchadnezzar, but it is certainly some extreme humour entirely at the king's expense! It is the opposite of personification (verse 32 above), so perhaps it should be labelled 'de-personification'?

Nebuchadnezzar's humiliation should also remind us of the trick that God played on Jacob in Genesis 29, when Jacob the Deceiver awoke, the morning after his wedding,

---

133 The temple sanctuary in 21:2

next to the wrong woman. Jacob was given a taste of God's sour providence; Nebuchadnezzar too learned the taste of humility before *God*.

And we must learn humility before our *God*. It is better to learn humility from scripture, but we all need a little help and, to do that, God often throws humiliating experiences into our lives. On these occasions, we need to remember Jacob, Nebuchadnezzar, and Hebrews 12-

- Hebrews 12:6 *...the Lord disciplines the one he loves, and he chastens everyone he accepts as his son.'* NIV

****

Figure 12: Rembrandt's Belshazzar's Feast.
Note the king with his eyes popping out at the riddle on the wall.
National Gallery. wikimedia commons, public domain.

A mildly humorous riddle is an integral part of the Samson story in Judges 14:12-19, and there are riddles in Proverbs, but the biblical use of a riddle reaches a new height in Daniel 5.

Belshazzar has a feast at which he irreverently and sacrilegiously uses gold and silver tableware from the temple of God in Jerusalem. Belshazzar knew all about how the one true God had dealt with his predecessor, Nebuchadnezzar (5:22).

So when Belshazzar not only drinks from the holy receptacles but even sings the praises of *gods of silver and gold*, that represents a direct challenge to the LORD himself. The initial divine response to Belshazzar is in the form of a riddle-

- Daniel 5:25 *'This is the inscription that was written:* MENE, MENE, TEKEL, PARSIN
  [26] *'Here is what these words mean:*
  Mene: God has numbered the days of your reign and brought it to an end.
  [27] *Tekel: You have been weighed on the scales and found wanting.*
  [28] *Peres: Your kingdom is divided and given to the Medes and Persians.'* NIV

Ironically, Belshazzar tries to pretend that there is nothing amiss, and clothes Daniel with royal purple etc. The very next verse, though, unceremoniously states-

- Daniel 5:30 *That very night Belshazzar, king of the Babylonians, was slain* NIV

The composer William Walton wrote an oratorio based on these events. At a party, he once conducted the choral shout of the single word, *"Slain"*, using a fly swatter. Belshazzar was the fly.

Such a summary execution throws divine scorn, perhaps the sharpest form of humour, at the king.

****

Daniel chapter 6 contains the memorable conundrum of the *law of the Medes and Persians*, which *can never be changed* (6:8). The newly appointed satraps (6:1) realise that they can only trap *Daniel* if they do something sneaky that involves a different law, the *law of his God-*

- Daniel 6:5 … *'We will never find any basis for charges against this man Daniel unless it has something to do with the law of his God.'* NIV

And so the stage is set for a 'shoot-out' between the *Law of God* and the *Law of the Medes and Persians*. That in itself is already quite funny for all biblical readers.

The satraps easily trick arrogant King Darius into making it illegal for *Daniel* to worship the true *God*. The king puts the new unchangeable *law* in writing; Daniel immediately breaks it by carrying on having his thrice daily quiet times, a practice which is uncomfortable to most of us.

Thus, *Daniel* is trapped and thrown into the lion's den (6:16). Or, rather, it is the king who is ironically trapped by his own proud *law*. We watch in pity as he reluctantly gives the order for *Daniel* to die (6:16); we almost feel sorry for him as he has a sleepless night (6:18). And we are impressed as he arrives at the lion's den very early next morning, greatly humbled-

- Daniel 6:20 *When he came near the den, he called to Daniel in an anguished voice, 'Daniel, servant of the living God, has your God, whom you serve continually, been able to rescue you from the lions?'* NIV

At the beginning of the chapter, he was the king-god, equipped with the unrepealable *Law of the Medes and Persians*. Now, conscience-smitten, he is confessing that both he and *Daniel* are entirely dependant upon the mercy of the one true and *living God, Daniel's God*. This is all very enjoyable for lovers of the *living God*.

Then the suspense turns into triumph, the pathos into vindication, and the irony into outright laughter, as the evil satraps get their comeuppance (6:24). Suddenly, we are reminded of the deadly seriousness of biblical humour-

- 6:24 *At the king's command, the men who had falsely accused Daniel were brought in and thrown into the lions' den, along with their wives and children. And before they reached the floor of the den, the lions overpowered them and crushed all their bones.* NIV

And so, we are not quite allowed to enjoy the joke, as those who were relatively innocent are also fed to the lions!

How serious the consequences of our own ill behaviour can be for our families. So often, we think that we are just weak Christians and merely feeble parents — nothing too serious. We only occasionally manage to set our children a good example. We rarely have Daniel-like self-discipline when it comes to having regular quiet times. Only occasionally do we teach them something biblical, comforting ourselves that it will be 'all right on the night'.

But, the truth is that all the time we are not devoted to God and his word, we are still teaching them by example: We are teaching them how unworthy our God is of their worship, and how unimportant his word is. In other words, we are teaching them '24/7'. What we do, what we don't do, how we do what we do do; these all have significant and eternal consequences for the next generation and for the other members of our families.

6. Humour in the Minor Prophets

There is very little explicit and obvious humour in the minor prophets, but the one exception, who stands out, is also the one who is the butt of the humour, Jonah. Let us examine them in the traditional order.

6.1 Hosea

If the book of Joshua uses Rahab the pagan prostitute to shame unbelieving Israel, then Hosea really goes to town. In order to shame, embarrass and humble his own people, *the LORD* commands Hosea to-

- Hosea 1:2 '*Go, marry a promiscuous woman and have children with her, for like an adulterous wife this land is guilty of unfaithfulness to the LORD.*' NIV

So rather than having Hosea visit everywhere and preach about their spiritual immorality, Hosea is given the job of acting it out, together with his family. The humour here is shocking, vulgar and aimed at provoking recognition by the Israelites that they are just like *Gomer*, Hosea's *adulterous wife*.

Recognition is a form of humour that we have previously seen deployed in 2 Chronicles (Ahab), Ezra and Proverbs. But Hosea takes the humour to a whole new level, by acting it out. We are familiar with spoof humour, e.g., '*the Star Ship Enterprise was now marooned in space, having been hit by tins of red and blue paint.*'[134] Does Hosea justify drama in church? I think not, no more than Hosea marrying an unrepentant prostitute is recommended by scripture. But Hosea does enable us to appreciate how our *unfaithfulness* is abhorrent to our God.

As Hosea lives his weird life with a prostitute wife, their children are given word-play names-

- Hosea 1:3 … *Gomer...and bore him a son.*
  *⁴ Then the LORD said to Hosea, 'Call him **Jezreel**, because I will soon punish the house of Jehu for the massacre at Jezreel, and I will put an end to the kingdom of Israel. ⁵ In that day I will break Israel's bow in the Valley of **Jezreel**.'*
  *⁶ Gomer conceived again and gave birth to a daughter. Then the LORD said to Hosea, 'Call her Lo-Ruhamah (which means "not **loved**"), for I will no longer show **love** to Israel, that I should at all forgive them.*

And yet, the spoof is also a romance-

---

134 *Star Turk*, BBC Radio 4.

- Hosea 1:7 *Yet I will show love to Judah; and I will save them — not by bow, sword or battle, or by horses and horsemen, but I, the LORD their God, will save them.'* NIV

Once again, if we tried to put the book of Hosea into practice by emulating the behaviour of Hosea or Gomer, we would come seriously unstuck. But if we recognise it as a kind of humour, a spoof play acted out, we will learn *wisdom-*

- Hosea 14:9 *Who is wise? Let them realise these things.*
  Who is discerning? Let them understand.
  The ways of the LORD are right;
  the righteous walk in them,
  but the rebellious stumble in them. NIV

****

Hosea also ridicules the ungodly people for relying on *Egypt*. He does this by likening Ephraim[135] to a *faulty* weapon-

- Hosea 7:16 *They do not turn to the Most High; they are like a faulty bow. Their leaders will fall by the sword because of their insolent words. For this they will be ridiculed in the land of Egypt.*

6.2 Joel

Joel is really not big on humour. However, he does make a lot of some promised locust plagues (1:4). The prophet appears to be employing 'shock' to remind the people of-

a) the plague of locusts that had previously devastated Egypt (Exodus 10),

b) an imminent invasion by actual locusts (1:4) and,

c) future judgements by the LORD (Joel 2ff).

6.3 Amos

Amos promises God's judgement on Judah and the surrounding nations. Again, the shock of a plague of locusts, that was narrowly averted, is employed to awaken Israel (7:1-6).

Then a surprising image is shown to *Amos*, that of a *plumb line* (7:7-9). There is no word-play here[136], but there is the suggestion that Israel were a

---

135 A way of referring to the northern kingdom of Israel.
136 Although there may be a 'sound-play'. See note 16 on Amos 7:7 in the NET Bible.

nation of 'cowboy builders'. From now on, *the LORD* is going to assess the quality of their work using the plumb line of his covenant law! They had probably never looked at things that way.

The element of surprise makes the lesson unforgettable, which is frequently a way in which humour is used in scripture. Nowadays, we are familiar with the idea of building inspectors who visit new buildings to check that building regulations have been complied with. In this way, the illegal high places[137] that they have been building (7:9) will be audited against God's standards, using God's *plumb line*.

In 7:17 the threat of prostitution is used again[138]. And then, Amos is given a word-play to emphasise just how *ripe* the *people* are for judgement-

- Amos 8:2 *'What do you see, Amos?' he asked. 'A basket of **ripe** fruit,' I answered. Then the LORD said to me, 'The time is **ripe** for my people Israel; I will spare them no longer.* NIV

Then there is another word-play[139], on the meaning of the word *'famine'*-

- Amos 8:11 *'The days are coming,' declares the Sovereign LORD,*
  *'when I will send a **famine** through the land—*
  *not a **famine** of food or a thirst for water,*
  *but a **famine** of hearing the words of the LORD.* NIV

This kind of humour has been deployed to show us that there are even worse kinds of *famine* than having no *food*: Being deprived of God's *word* is the ultimate famine, when his *word* of wisdom is taken away, his *word* of providence is withheld, his *word* of blessing is absent. Such a threat must surely serve warn to us nowadays too.

Then the mood changes, and *Amos* gives a beautiful, paradoxical, almost comical, picture of future days of God's blessing-

- Amos 9:13 ...*'when the reaper will be overtaken by the ploughman*
  and the planter by the one treading grapes. NIV

Idolaters will never be seen again, but King David's successor, the Messiah, will bring abundant blessing. Now that we live under Jesus' new covenant, we too should expect[140] blessing, harvest and fruitfulness.

---

137 Raised places of pagan and idolatrous worship
138 See Hosea, previously herein.
139 This may even count as a riddle, but the riddle is immediately explained in the same verse.
140 But certainly not presume

6.4 Obadiah

Obadiah is entirely about God's judgement on the nation of Edom for their hostility to their cousins[141], the descendants of Jacob. The subject does not sound humorous, and it isn't, but some of the detail utilises surprising imagery of a humorous kind-

- Obadiah 5 *'If thieves came to you,*
  if robbers in the night –
  oh, what a disaster awaits you –
  would they not steal only as much as they wanted?
  If grape pickers came to you,
  would they not leave a few grapes?' NIV

So you think that you will just be mildly rebuked by God, do you? Oh no, the tables will be completely turned! Just as you gloated over Israel, so the LORD will *gloat* over you-

- Obadiah 12 *You should not gloat over your brother[110]*
  in the day of his misfortune,
  nor rejoice over the people of Judah
  in the day of their destruction, NIV

Even gloating is a type of humour.

6.5 Jonah

So far, the minor prophets have looked rather tenuous candidates for using humour. However, Jonah is wall-to-wall humour from beginning to end.

There is the mad prophet of the one true God, who imagines that he can flee from God's presence (Cf. Psalm 139:7-12)! God's omnipresence is taught in an understated[142], clear, but ridiculous way, as Jonah tries to evade his God.

There is the remarkable providence of a ship for Jonah at the port of Joppa. How that wreaks havoc with our notions of divine guidance! The word of God should always be our first port of call when we need guidance, not convenience, nor preconceived desires.

---

141 Referred to as their brother in verses 10 and 12.
142 Litotes or Meiosis

There is the surprisingly Christ-like way that Jonah is asleep in the stern[143] while a storm threatens to sink the ship (1:5); then there is the irony that Jonah, the only one with a real God, is the only one not calling on him (1:6) for help.

There is a Christlike sacrifice[144] as they throw the guilty prophet overboard to calm the storm. At the same time, we see the strange irony that here is a prophet whose behaviour is anything but Christlike![145]

Then the sailors all seem to be converted without Jonah trying to evangelise[146] them at all (1:14-16).

Chapter 2 has God's prophetic mouthpiece getting fishier and fishier until he partially repents, vows to preach in Nineveh, and gets vomited out by the big fish. All this is the comic combined with the vulgar[147]. And yet, amidst it all, Jonah utters one of the greatest theological statements ever[148]-

- Jonah 2:9 ... *"Salvation comes from the LORD."*

It would be worth it all just to hear that summary of God's dealings with humanity, and yet it is all presented to us in the middle of a laugh-out-loud story of God humiliating his unwilling prophet with a fish. Why does such profound theology come to us all mixed up with divine humour?

The supposedly penitent prophet goes to *Nineveh* and preaches the most inadequate gospel sermon ever-

- Jonah 3:4 ... *'Forty more days and Nineveh will be overthrown.'*

And, to his horror (4:1), they all repent, and *the LORD* forgives them.

Then to crown it all, God smites Jonah's beloved plant (4:7) to show Jonah that he actually cares more about the plant than all the people in *Nineveh*. As if somehow that wasn't the ultimate combination of pathos and humour, God then adds that Jonah did not even care about *'the many animals'* in Nineveh, never mind the 120,000 souls (4:11). Now that is unforgettable sarcasm, not to mention uncomfortable for all of us plant-lovers!

Thus, Jonah's idolatry of his own Jewish nationalism, expressed in his unconditional hatred of the Ninevites, is left hanging there in the air. It challenges all of us readers

---

143 Mark 4:38
144 Matthew 12:40
145 Matthew 5:44
146 In fact, Jonah previously seems to have done the very opposite of evangelism in 1:10.
147 Small children love Jonah 2:10.
148 The late theologian, Ed Clowney calls it the statement that summarises the whole Bible.

about our own idols that we stubbornly refuse to make bow[149] to the one true, international, God.

Anyone not laughing out loud at the book of Jonah should check his pulse urgently. Again, it is a case of humour being used to generate recognition of our own attitudes. Did the Ninevites need to repent of all the impaling etc. that they were famous for?[150] Absolutely.

Figure 13: Impalement of Judeans in a Neo-Assyrian relief, ME 124906 in British Museum.

---

149 Like Dagon, 1 Samuel 5:4
150 https://en.wikipedia.org/wiki/Nineveh accessed 01/07/2019. Some have pointed out that maybe the impaling happened only after the victims were dead, so I suppose that's all right then.

Did Jonah need to repent of his hateful attitude to his enemies? Jesus certainly taught us so (Matthew 5:44). Do we need to repent of our attitude to evil Oxbridge atheists, Charles Darwin, the Pope, godless legislators in government today, anti-theistic educators, BBC Radio 4, insert your most-hated enemy here? We should be praying for our enemies and the enemies of God's kingdom.

6.6 Micah

Micah uses some of the starkest language in scripture against the godless northern and southern kingdoms of Judah and Samaria-

- Micah 3:1 *Then I said, 'Listen, you leaders of Jacob, you rulers of Israel.*
  Should you not embrace justice,
  ² you who hate good and love evil;
  who tear the skin from my people and the flesh from their bones;
  ³ who eat my people's flesh, strip off their skin and break their bones in pieces;
  who chop them up like meat for the pan, like flesh for the pot.' NIV

Such ghastly figures of speech are typical of Micah. If this is humour, it is of the sickening, gory, incongruous sort. Is this the kind of *'gross out'* humour that appeals to pre-adolescent boys which we noticed in Judges? Well, it certainly paints a revolting picture of Israel's leaders as butchers! Such extreme incongruity may not be the kind of humour that we enjoy, and, of course, it was never intended for enjoyment, but for rebuke.

In complete contrast, the same book contains an explicit prediction of where a new, gentle and godly, ruler will be born: Bethlehem[151]; and he will-

- Micah 5:4 ... *stand and shepherd his flock in the strength of the* LORD...

It is significant that the best leaders of God's people are often referred to in the Bible as *shepherds* (not butchers). See Amos 1:1; Acts 20:28; 1 Peter 5:2. Brothers, we have high standards to live up to as under-shepherds, and as those who have been given to the flock by the *chief-shepherd*[152]-

- Ephesians 4:11 *And he gave the apostles, the prophets, the evangelists, the shepherds and teachers...* ESV

---

151 Micah 5:2; Contrast *Doeg* the butcher-*shepherd* in 1 Samuel 21:7 with *King David* the *shepherd*-king.
152 1 Peter 5:4

6.7 Nahum

Previously, we noticed the humour in the book of Jonah. Nahum also prophesied to the city of Nineveh. Although Nahum was probably one or two hundred years later than Jonah, can we nevertheless expect humour dangling like low hanging fruit in Nahum? No, but there is some: Nahum is full of striking imagery (e.g. 3:1-4). The LORD taunts Nineveh in her desolation-

- Nahum 2:11 *Where now is the lions' den,*
    the place where they fed their young,
  where the lion and lioness went,
    and the cubs, with nothing to fear?
  ¹² The lion killed enough for his cubs
    and strangled the prey for his mate,
  filling his lairs with the kill
    and his dens with the prey. NIV

And all Nineveh's victims *clap their hands* at its demise-

- Nahum 3:19 … *All who hear the news about you clap their hands at your fall,* …

Humour is not for use everywhere. There is a time and a place for everything, including humour[153].

6.8 Habakkuk

Habakkuk is full of famous statements, e.g. 1:13; 2:4c; 2:6b; 2:14.20; 3:17-18, which are used in hymns and other literature. It is reminiscent of Job and Jeremiah, in that it contains a pair of complaints but, unlike Job and Jeremiah, Habakkuk gets divine answers to his complaints. He goes up into his *watchtower* (2:1) to await *the LORD's* answers.

Habakkuk's first question is basically, "*LORD*, why don't you do something about ungodly Judeans?" *The LORD's* answer is that he will; he is going to bring the Babylonians to punish his own guilty people, the Babylonians who are so ferocious that they *laugh* at mere obstacles-

- Habakkuk 1:10 *They mock kings*
    and scoff at rulers.

---

153 Ecclesiastes 3:3 …*a time to tear down and a time to build, ⁴ a time to weep and a time to laugh*

They laugh at all fortified cities;
by building earthen ramps they capture them. NIV

Notice the humorous words, *'mock'*, *'scoff'* and *'laugh'*. This is how the Babylonians are, even when they are working for *the LORD*!

So Habakkuk's complaint then becomes, "How can you let the even-less-righteous Babylonians destroy the quite unrighteous Judeans?" *The LORD's* answer is that the Persians[154] will, in turn, bring the Babylonians to justice. As the Babylonians *laughed* at Judah, so the Persians will *laugh* at them-

- Habakkuk 2:6 *'Will not all of them taunt him with ridicule and scorn, ...'*

Habakkuk then ends with a psalm praising *the LORD* for his sovereignty in chapter 3. The song recalls God's anger at Egypt during the exodus-

- Habakkuk 3:8 *Were you angry with the rivers, LORD?*
  Was your wrath against the streams?
  Did you rage against the sea...?

Was it the personified waters who sinned, and not Pharaoh, who provoked *the LORD* to violence against mere water?

Habakkuk 2 contains five *'Woes'*. These use colourful language and metaphors-

- Habakkuk 2:9 *'Woe to him who builds his house by unjust gain...'*
  ...
  11 *The stones of the wall will cry out,*
  and the beams of the woodwork will echo it.

Here, the building materials themselves are personified, and they *cry out* at the builders' behaviour. Such personification is similar to the humour in Ezekiel where he addresses inanimate objects.[155]

Habakkuk laughs at idols in the same way as Isaiah[156] does-

- Habakkuk 2:19 *Woe to him who says to wood,*
  "Come to life!"
  Or to lifeless stone,
  "Wake up!" NIV

We are nearly at the end of the Old Testament. The Old Covenant is in tatters, the Davidic Covenant, ruined. The prophets are in serious danger of being repetitive.

---

154 Although, not named in Habakkuk.
155 Ezekiel 6:2; 20:46; 35:2, 36:2; 37:4
156 Isaiah 44

If I look at the contents page in a Bible, I can see that the major prophets begin on page 1,000 and continue for roughly another 400 pages, through to the end of the minor prophets. Almost all prophets are saying the same things: Stop, repent, turn, judgement, exile. We have to make sure that we learn from everything that happened before Jesus came to make sure that we do not unwittingly repeat it all-

- 1 Corinthians 10:6 *Now these things occurred as examples to keep us from setting our hearts on evil things as they did.*

6.9 Zephaniah

Zephaniah is a short version of Isaiah. Like Isaiah, it contains a set of judgements against the various nations whom *the* LORD had used to chastise Judah. First, Moab and Ammon will be repaid for their wrong use of humour-

- Zephaniah 2:10 *This is what they will get in return for their pride, for insulting and mocking the people of the* LORD *Almighty.* NIV

Next, the Assyrians are *scoffed* at for engaging in blasphemous boasting[157]-

- Zephaniah 2:15 *This is the city of revelry
    that lived in safety.
    She said to herself,
        'I am the one! And there is none besides me.'
    What a ruin she has become,
        a lair for wild beasts!
    All who pass by her scoff
        and shake their fists.* NIV

---
157 Deuteronomy 32:39 '*See now that I myself am he! There is no god besides me*'

But before all that, do you remember *Dagon,* who so humorously bowed low before the ark of the LORD in 1 Samuel 5? After that, *Dagon* seemed to make a recovery, and stood victorious over King Saul in 1 Chronicles 10, where we left him for a while-

- 1 Chronicles 10:10 *They put his* [Saul's] *armour in the temple of their gods and hung up his head in the temple of Dagon.*

Did Dagon have the last laugh over God's idolatrous people in full view of the uncircumcised Philistines? No, because in Zephaniah 1, we see that *Dagon* is unable to protect his priests from finally being punished by *the LORD-*

- Zephaniah 1:9 *On that day I will punish all who avoid 'stepping on the threshold',* ... i.e. *Dagon's* priests; see 1 Samuel 5:5.

It may take hundreds of years, but *the LORD* never forgets his enemies, and always remembers his people. And where events are recorded humorously in the Bible, he will always have the last laugh. It may sometimes appear to God's people that *Dagon* is still standing, but in the end he will always let down his servants. Idols are cruel masters and unreliable gods.

6.10 Haggai

Despite being the second smallest book in the Hebrew Bible, Haggai nevertheless has room for a little humour. It is not laugh-out-loud humour, but the LORD asks a series of questions through the prophet to make the people think. The people were amongst the 50,000 or so who had returned to Judah to rebuild Jerusalem and, in particular, the temple of God-

- Haggai 1:4 *'Is it a time for you yourselves to be living in your panelled houses, while this house remains a ruin?'* NIV

Now the temple was not precisely *a ruin,* so this is mild hyperbole, but it was only half finished. Work had stopped roughly a decade earlier, but now there was no excuse; Zerubbabel must recommence the building work; a new king, Darius, had authorised the work to resume[158].

Another challenging hyperbole appears in chapter 2-

- Haggai 2:3 *"Who of you is left who saw this house in its former glory? How does it look to you now? Does it not seem to you like nothing?"* NIV

---

158 Ezra 6:12

Really, *nothing*? But this time, the hyperbole is accompanied by divine promises and encouragements to be strong, because *the LORD is with* them (2:4).

However, some rebuke is still needed-

- Haggai 2:13 *Then Haggai said, 'If a person defiled by contact with a dead body touches one of these things, does it become defiled?'* NIV

The question must have seemed ridiculous, even comically simplistic, to the priests, who answered, "Yes". *Haggai* then goes on to explain that there is an equally obvious connection between obedience and blessing. If they want God to bless them, they must obey him[159].

For us too, although blessing comes to us only through God's grace[160], there is still normally a straightforward connection between us obeying and him blessing. The ordinary means of grace[161] can be ignored by us so easily. At first, we do not notice the lack of blessing. But this is, say, because we weren't there[162] when everyone else received the blessings of fellowship, the reading and preaching of God's word, the sacraments. But if we still do not obey (this, for example),-

- Hebrews 10:24 *And let us consider how we may spur one another on towards love and good deeds,* [25] *not giving up meeting together, as some are in the habit of doing, but encouraging one another…* NIV

Then not only do we miss out on the obvious *encouragement*, but God, our Father, starts to 'turn the wick up', and chastises us. If we do not fear God chastising[163] us, then we obviously do not fear God, and that is serious.

6.11 Zechariah

Zechariah has virtually no narrative, and is an apocalyptic book like Daniel and Revelation are, so there is not much opportunity for humour. But Zechariah was working alongside Haggai to exhort the people to restart rebuilding the temple, and uses the same penetrating questions, some humorous, to examine the people's heart-motivations-

---

159 Under the Old Covenant and the Davidic Covenant, the connection was especially obvious because of all the outward ordinances, e.g. the physical temple, the promised land etc.
160 And actually, the same grace was needed in 520BC.
161 See Westminster Shorter Catechism 1646/7 Q.88
162 Like Thomas Didymus in John 20:24
163 Hebrews 12:4-11

- Zechariah 1:5 *'Where are your ancestors now? And the prophets, do they live for ever? ⁶ But did not my words and my decrees, which I commanded my servants the prophets, overtake your ancestors?'* NIV

Where were their *ancestors*? Dead, in Sheol. You can run (like Jonah) but you cannot escape from God's *words*. This is shocking sarcasm that invites them to recognise themselves as being just as bad as their *ancestors*.

Some parts of Zechariah seem funny to us but were probably not intended to be at all funny originally, for example-

- Zechariah 1:18 *Then I looked up, and there before me were four horns. ¹⁹ I asked the angel who was speaking to me, 'What are these?'* NIV

Horns are actually perfectly normal in apocalyptic literature, and represent kings and emperors, as symbols of power.

However, in chapter 7, the people ask Zechariah if they should still keep fasting. The LORD's reply contains this rather sarcastic comment-

- Zechariah 7:6 *'And when you were eating and drinking, were you not just feasting for yourselves?'* NIV

Thus, some ironic criticism cuts straight through the people's empty religious acts.

In chapter 8, Zechariah presents the people with an image of eternal bliss, in Jerusalem, which presumably represents the new Jerusalem one day on the new Earth. *The LORD Almighty* adds-

- Zechariah 8:6 *...'It may seem marvellous to the remnant of this people at that time, but will it seem marvellous to me?'* NIV

God can see the future, but the people of Jerusalem can only see the current difficulties. But a little wit helps to lighten the mood and make the prophecy easier to accept. With God, it is possible.[164]

Zechariah 13 contains a prediction about false prophets. One day false prophets will be removed. If any are left, their families will *stab* them! (13:3) So, they will all pretend to be *farmers* to avoid being stabbed any more. Then, we read-

- Zechariah 13:6 *'If someone asks, "What are these wounds on your body?" they will answer, "The wounds I was given at the house of my friends."'* NIV

Somehow the *stab wounds* were a good thing, because they ended the false prophesying, and caused the ex-prophets to take up a wholesome occupation

---

164 Luke 18:27

(farming). The juxtapositioning of *wounds* and *friends* is intriguing and at least a little humorous. The ex-prophet seems to be saying, in a shocking way, that those who stabbed him did him a favour!

6.12 Malachi

Malachi denounces many of the same sins amongst the recently-returned people as Nehemiah did. He caricatures the people as those who keep asking questions in seeming wide-eyed, childish, innocence-

- Malachi 1:2 … '*But you ask, "How have you loved us?"*'

- Malachi 1:6 … '*But you ask, "How have we shown contempt for your name?"*'

- Malachi 1:7 … '*But you ask, "How have we defiled you?"*' [165]

To that last, idiotic, question, the answer is-

- Malachi 1:8 '… *When you sacrifice lame or diseased animals, is that not wrong?*
  Try offering them to your governor! Would he be pleased with you?'

The explanation above is quite sarcastic. It pretends that they are stupid enough to think that the LORD's eyesight is inferior to that of their *governor*! But they monotonously continue, on and on, like a 'cracked record'-[166]

- Malachi 2:17 … '*How have we wearied him?*' NIV

- Malachi 3:7 … '*But you ask, "How are we to return?"*'

- Malachi 3:8 … '*But you ask, "How are we robbing you?"*'

In fact, God seems utterly sick of his disingenuous people-

- Malachi 1:10 '*Oh, that one of you would shut the temple doors,*
  so that you would not light useless fires on my altar!
  I am not pleased with you,' NIV

God also seems to be so patient with his annoying people, but he saves a bit of vulgar, almost slap-stick, humour specially for the priests, who surely ought to know better than the commoners-

---

165 I know; this is getting annoying already, and you are just the reading about it.

166 A word of explanation for millennials and Generation Z: Your parents used to listen to music cut into vinyl discs. These were called 'records'. If damaged, the music would sometimes jump back a bit and repeat the same music over and over again.

- Malachi 2:3 *'Because of you I will rebuke your descendants; I will smear on your faces the dung from your festival sacrifices...'* NIV

And that is how the humour in the Hebrew Bible ends — with a wearying, sinful, people, and their God who is *wearied* with them. The questioning continues-

- Malachi 2:17 ...*'Where is the God of justice?'*

That facile question comes from the lips of a sinful people, implying that somehow God is at fault! And yet, if the *God of justice* had been anything less than incredibly merciful, they would surely have been destroyed generations ago!

7. Humour in the Apocrypha?

If you are from a High Anglican, Roman Catholic or Orthodox Church background, you may have been taught that the Old Testament Apocryphal books are 'scripture', that is, part of the Bible. However, these books were written in the last few centuries BC and have never been considered to be scripture by the Hebrews, by the early church, nor by Protestants in general.

As can be seen from the King James or Authorised Version contents page above, the Apocryphal books have sometimes been associated with scripture, but are not themselves God-breathed.[167] They contain material that flatly contradicts scripture, for example-

- Tobit 12: 8b *It is better to give alms than to lay up gold:*
  [9] For alms doth deliver from death, and shall purge away all sin. KJV 1611

The Apocrypha also contain humour, but what is interesting is how apocryphal humour sometimes differs from biblical humour. Now often, the humour is very similar to biblical humour, consisting of puns, word-plays and tales that deride false gods-

- Bel and the Dragon[168] 3 '*Now the Babylonians had an idol, called Bel, and there were spent upon him every day twelve great measures of fine flour, and forty sheep, and six vessels of wine. [4] And the king worshipped it and went daily to adore it: but Daniel worshipped his own God. And the king said unto him, Why dost not thou worship Bel? [5] Who answered and said, Because I may not worship idols made with hands, but the living God, who hath created the heaven and the earth, and hath sovereignty over all flesh. [6] Then said the king unto him, Thinkest thou not that Bel is a living God? Seest thou not how much he eateth and drinketh every day?'* KJV 1611

Bel subsequently gets demoted when it is discovered that it is his priests, and their families, rather than the god, who are the ones with the large diurnal appetites![169]

---

167 Theopneustos (θεόπνευστος) in 2 Timothy 3:16 means 'breathed out by God', not 'inspired'.

168 *Bel and the Dragon* consists of a single witty chapter.

169 Indeed, it is really rather funny that pagan gods seem to need to be fed. The Gilgamesh epic includes an account where the gods almost starve to death because nobody fed them. Poor gods, but maybe the top god, Enlil, should have known better and not flooded the world?

But sometimes the humour has a very different flavour. In *Tobit*, one, *Tobias*, remembers some previously received 'wisdom', ...

- Tobit 8:2b ... *and took the ashes of the perfumes, and put the heart and the liver of the fish thereupon, and made a smoke therewith. ³ The which smell when the evil spirit had smelled, he fled into the utmost parts of Egypt, and the angel bound him.* KJV 1611

Now that goes beyond our previously identified biblical categories of humour[170]; instead of the ridiculous and the absurd, we now have the plain stupid, the-beyond-the-pale, and the contradictory. The possessed woman is not affected by the terrible odour, but an evil spirit is?

Previously *Tobit* has been made blind-

- Tobit 2:9 *The same night also I returned from the burial, and slept by the wall of my courtyard, being polluted and my face was uncovered: ¹⁰ And I knew not that there were sparrows in the wall, and mine eyes being open, the sparrows muted warm dung into mine eyes, and a whiteness came in mine eyes: and I went to the physicians, but they helped me not ...* KJV 1611

Now that would certainly constitute a unique piece of biblical humour if it had been biblical, not to mention a very strange way to go blind! Leonard Greenspoon comments-

'Elsewhere there are also comedic moments, possibly inserted to relieve the tension of the narrative.' [171]

If he is right, then such a use of apocryphal humour is very different from how the Bible uses humour. The Bible uses humour at its most serious points, at the climax of its narratives. Think, for example, of the way that the Egyptian gods are defeated one by one during the exodus narrative. The apocrypha, however, feel the need to insert some light relief to make the story less intense!

****

The book of *Judith* starts off with a mass of historical errors (Judith 1:1-5). Greenspoon takes these as plainly advertising that a humorous story is to follow-

'The author of Judith intentionally and with humorous effect sets out these inaccuracies to let readers know that what follows is not to be understood as a sober account'

He was a god after all.

170 See the box containing categories of humour in the introduction.

171 https://global.oup.com/obso/focus/focus_on_humor_apocrypha/ accessed 24/06/2019 OUP America.

Again, if he is right[172], this is not how the Bible uses historical data. For example, the apostle John, in his eye-witness account and gospel, includes lots of historical recollections of detail in order to authenticate his account. For example, John records the facts that the high priest's servant in John 18 was called *Malchus,* and that it was his *right ear* that Peter cut off (18:10).

****

It is interesting how even the style of the Apocrypha seems to differ from scripture. The confusingly named, single chapter, *Letter of Jeremiah,* appears at first to be deriding idols in a thoroughly biblical way, but then it says-

- Letter of Jeremiah 21 *Their* [idols'] *faces are blacked through the smoke that cometh out of the temple.* [22] *Upon their bodies and heads sit bats, swallows, and birds, and the cats also.* KJV 1611

The mention of *bats* and *cats*, whilst certainly funny in a rather biblical way, makes the text appear alien to actual scripture, perhaps derivative, but definitely fitting a different and non-canonical ecosystem.

In this way, we can compare apocryphal humour with biblical humour, and with the categories of biblical humour in the introduction, and see for ourselves that the Apocrypha, though undoubtedly funny, also appear phoney.

8. Humour in the Gospels

The synoptic gospels[173] share a lot of their humour, particularly when it is on the lips of Jesus. But each gospel also has its own special blend, which makes it well worthwhile taking each gospel separately. John's gospel is very different from the synoptics.

8.1 Matthew

Matthew's gospel starts with a bang — Jesus is not only the Messiah, but is also descended from both *David* and *Abraham*. Any Christian Jew should surely stand tall and enjoy an introduction like this-

- Matthew 1:1 *This is the genealogy of Jesus the Messiah*[174]
  the son of David,
  the son of Abraham.

---

172 And I think he probably is. But, if he is wrong, the errors serve to undermine the status of the Apocrypha still further.
173 Matthew, Mark and Luke, which all share a similar viewpoint, hence 'synoptic'.
174 NIV; Christ, χριστος in Greek

But then, something funny happens. It turns out that *Jesus* has some rather dodgy ancestors, such as *Judah* in verse 2. Was he not the one who used his own daughter-in-law as a prostitute and then tried to burn her to death?[175] And then (verse 5), *Ruth* is mentioned; wasn't she a woman?[176] And a Moabite, descended from Lot by an incestuous act?[177]

Many years ago, we had a home group, and were studying Genesis. One member of the group, recently converted from the world, was rather shocked by the behaviour of Jesus' ancestors as recorded in Genesis! She was right to be shocked.

Still in only verse 5 of chapter 1, we have *Rahab*, the gentile pagan prostitute. And why is *Uriah the Hittite* mentioned in verse 6? Oh yes, *King David* stole his wife and then got *Uriah* murdered! Then, there is that long list of kings after *David* from verse 7 down to 11: There were some really rather nasty characters amongst that shower! For example, take King *Manasseh*: He even sacrificed his own children by burning them alive to a pagan god[178]. OK, Matthew, you can stop now. We understand that you wrote your gospel purely to humiliate, shock and cause permanent emotional damage to your Jewish readers!

And yet, though the list is humbling and troubling, the actual punch line is-

*   Matthew 1:21 *She* [Mary] *will give birth to a son,*
    and you are to give him the name Jesus, [the LORD saves]
    because he will save his people from their sins.'

Before introducing *Jesus* the saviour, Matthew has introduced us to some of the people he came to *save from their sins.* They are sinful people, those who *need a 'doctor'*[179], those who needed a saviour hundreds of years before he even came.

Such an opening is a great encouragement to both Jews and Gentiles to come to such a saviour, in our sin, and rely on the one who came to *save* such sinful *people from their sins.* That combination of shocking, shameful, humiliating humour, and absolutely vital gospel truth about Jesus' origins is profound. We are again reminded of how the Bible reserves its humour for very special occasions indeed, in this case, for Christmas.

****

---

175 Genesis 38:24
176 This may not shock us, but it would certainly have made Matthew's original readers sit up and take notice!
177 Genesis 19:30-37
178 2 Kings 21, 2 Chronicles 33
179 Matthew 9:12

In Matthew 2, Herod the Great (37BC to 4BC) discovers from the magi that a new king has been born. He tricks the magi into going to Bethlehem to find Jesus and then come back and tell him. The naïve trick fails (2:12), so Herod immediately kills all the toddlers in Bethlehem. Here we have evil Herod's trickery juxtaposed with a major act of infanticide. We are glad when he dies in verse 19.

****

So far, Matthew's humour has not always been enjoyable, but in chapter 3, John the baptist insults some hypocrites-

- Matthew 3:7 ... '*You brood of vipers!*
   Who warned you to flee from the coming wrath?
   ⁸ Produce fruit in keeping with repentance.' NIV

Here, humour of a sharp kind reveals a major theme in Matthew's gospel: That we must at all costs avoid being hypocrites as the Pharisee *vipers* were, as Jesus himself puts it in the sermon on the mount-

- Matthew 5:20 *For I tell you that unless your righteousness surpasses*
   that of the Pharisees and the teachers of the law,
   you will certainly not enter the kingdom of heaven. NIV

That statement in itself would have been laughable to some of Jesus' hearers. Weren't the *Pharisees* the super-holy ones? How can we possibly be more *righteous* than they? By not being hypocrites.

Furthermore, when there is a risk of people failing to *enter the kingdom of heaven*, Jesus does not shrink back from using an insult to make the crucial point.

****

In Matthew 4 there is a lovely and memorable word play on *fish* and *fishermen-*

- Matthew 4:18 *As Jesus was walking beside the Sea of Galilee, he saw*
   two brothers, Simon called Peter and his brother Andrew. They were
   *casting a net into the lake, for they were **fishermen**.*
   ¹⁹ 'Come, follow me,' Jesus said,
   *'and I will send you out to **fish** for people.'*
   ²⁰ At once they left their nets
   and followed him. NIV

Although the new disciples might have been mystified at the time, they nevertheless dropped their *nets and followed* Jesus. Impressive and memorable. Perhaps only some time later did they realise what Jesus had meant[180]. Such a great example, made so memorable by Jesus' fishers-of-men pun, illustrates how important it is for us obey Jesus even if we do not fully understand yet. We must trust first, obey next, and the understanding can come later.

****

In Matthew 5, Jesus uses a radical blend of humour to make his punchy teaching totally memorable and unsettling-

- Matthew 5:3 '*Blessed are the poor in spirit,*
      for theirs is the kingdom of heaven.
   4 Blessed are those who mourn,
      for they will be comforted.
   5 Blessed are the meek,
      for they will inherit the earth. NIV
   ...

   11 'Blessed are you when people insult you, persecute you and falsely say all kinds of evil against you because of me. 12 Rejoice and be glad, because great is your reward in heaven, for in the same way they persecuted the prophets who were before you.' NIV

How would the Beatitudes initially have struck Matthew's readers? The initial word, Μακάριοι=Makarioi[181], would simply have struck them as meaning 'happy'. But this is no temporary or fleeting feeling of happiness, so translators usually use the word '*blessed*' instead. The first three beatitudes in particular contain apparent contradictions-

(5:3) "You can be *truly happy* even if you are either literally *poor* (because of your devotion to Jesus as per v12), or even if you are not literally poor (but nevertheless have an attitude that is *poor in spirit*), because you own *the kingdom of heaven.*"

(5:4) "You can be *truly happy* even if you are currently *mourning* the death of someone near to you. How? Because you will be *comforted* and supported by the Paraclete[182], the Holy Spirit."

---

180 As per John 14:26

181 Leaving aside for the moment complication that Jesus probably said it in Aramiac, not Greek. See later on Matthew 23:24.

182 The Greek word for 'comforted' (παρακληθήσονται) here is related to one that is used by Jesus as recorded in John 14:16 to refer to the Holy Spirit's comforting or advocating rôle. It has a whole range

(5:5) "You can be *truly happy* even though you are so *meek* that people trample all over you because, actually you will *inherit the* whole *earth*, just as God promised Abraham[183]." And so on.

So the beatitudes are examples of Jesus pairing apparently contradictory ideas (poverty and wealth; sadness and consolation; meekness and greatness), and then releasing the tension between each pair by making a wonderful promise-

- [11] *'Blessed are you when people insult you...because great is your reward in heaven...*

When we finish reading the beatitudes, we might be frowning because of the poverty, mourning, meekness and insults, but we could be smiling because of the promised *kingdom, comfort, inheriting the earth,* and *great reward in heaven.* If the latter, then we 'got' the humour!

****

The sermon on the mount contains many startling images and commands, and even this short sketch-

- Matthew 5:23 *'Therefore, if you are offering your gift at the altar and there remember that your brother or sister has something against you,* [24] *leave your gift there in front of the altar. First go and be reconciled to them; then come and offer your gift.'* NIV

In this succinct reality play, we are temple worshippers. We witness some bizarre behaviour, where some-one, abruptly and for no apparent reason, dumps his offering, and rushes out of the temple.

Then, we realise that Jesus has ambushed us and is addressing us directly, "*First,* you *go and be reconciled*". The urgency for brothers to be at peace[184] is communicated humorously; the extreme behaviour emphasises its importance.

The subsequent section in the sermon on the mount, about adultery, was covered in the introduction.

****

---

of possible meanings.
183 Romans 4:13
184 Psalm 133:1

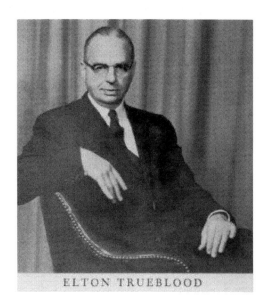
ELTON TRUEBLOOD

As we saw in the introduction, Elton Trueblood, in his book, '*The Humor of Christ*', finds thirty different humorous passages, not counting the duplicates in two or more gospels. His first one is the example of, what he calls, '*Automatic rewards*'[185] in Matthew 6:2,5,16-

- Matthew 6:2 '*So when you give to the needy,
    do not announce it with trumpets, as the hypocrites do...* NIV

You can almost see the smiles appearing on the faces of the ordinary people when Jesus makes that statement. He pulls no punches. He is dealing with a profoundly serious subject — hypocrisy. To make it punchy and memorable he uses overt sarcasm against the alms-giving Pharisees for the benefit of his disciples, who must, at all costs, avoid being *hypocrites*.

One wonders just how subjective the appreciation of humour is, because Trueblood appears to skip over the next obvious(?) example[186]-

- Matthew 5:15[187] *Neither do people light a lamp and put it under a bowl.* NIV

Here, Jesus paints a funny picture for us to laugh at, but then applies it to the subject of letting our own *light* shine, that is, our *good deeds* that bring *glory to* our *Father in heaven* (verse 16). This verse sits uncomfortably for many Evangelicals who are suspicious of a merely social gospel.

---
185 ...but rewards received only from the immediate human observers
186 Although it is alluded to on page 18 of *The Humor of Christ*.
187 Mark 4:21 features a *lamp under a bowl or bed*, but the use of humour is very similar.

Trueblood calls Matthew 6:34, '*No need to borrow trouble[188]*'-

- Matthew 6:34 *Therefore do not worry about tomorrow,*
  for tomorrow will worry about itself.
  Each day has enough trouble of its own. NIV [189]

Jesus' wry comment is made humorously because, frankly, we easily forget the Father's love and replace it with *worry*. There is *no need to borrow* some extra *trouble* to make up for a shortage today! The humour is partly comic understatement and partly just absurdity. It is, in fact, a verse with not one, but two, humorous ideas-

1. The simple statement, '*Tomorrow will worry about itself*' is a light-hearted personification to help us to '*laugh at the days to come*' like the virtuous wife in Proverbs 31:25.

2. The concise phrase, '*enough trouble of its own*' is understatement, aimed at helping us to focus on just the imminent problems of life.

In the same way that Jesus talks about hell more than anyone else in scripture, so he also makes use of humour freely and frequently.

****

There are a number of humorous passages that only occur in Matthew's gospel.[190] One is the pearls before swine parable-

- Matthew 7:6 '*Do not give dogs what is sacred;*
  do not throw your pearls to pigs.
    If you do, they may trample them under their feet,
  and turn and tear you to pieces.' NIV

Here, an amusing and ridiculous piece of generosity is then suddenly turned into a warning about how dangerous the Pharisees can be.

Some have perverted this parable to mean that we should never share the gospel with people unless they show some evidence that their hearts have first been made receptive by the Holy Spirit[191]. But that is to read far too much into the parable. Whilst Christians are required to take up their

---

188 ...from the future so that you can worry about it today. Trueblood p59
189 Notice also, how it is helpful to lay out some of these sayings as if they were in the book of Proverbs.
190 6:2,5,16; 7:6; 10:25; 15:14; 16:18; 18:28; 23:3,5,27
191 This is the spirit of hypercalvinism.

crosses and suffer with Jesus, there is no point stirring up a hornets' nest, nor of provoking hatred, insults or rebuke, from *mockers*. Discernment is wisdom-

- Proverbs 9:7 *Whoever corrects a mocker invites insults;*
  whoever rebukes the wicked incurs abuse. NIV

****

Much of the humour in the gospels is reserved for the Scribes[192] and Pharisees, but some of it is intended more generally, for any who persecute Jesus' people-

- Matthew 10:25 *It is enough for students to be like their teachers,*
  and servants like their masters.
  If the head of the house has been called Beelzebul,
  how much more the members of his household!
  [26] *'So do not be afraid of them, ...* NIV

Here[193] Jesus combines a justified insult of persecutors, with the warning that people in the devil's family will obviously persecute us. Rather than being *afraid*, we must rely on the Father's care. The day of judgement is coming; they will get their just deserts; you have eternal life.

****

Matthew 11 has Jesus talking about *John* the baptist. First, there is some mildly humorous understatement[194] of John the baptist's significance expressed as questions-

- Matthew 11:7 ... *'What did you go out into the wilderness to see?*
  A reed swayed by the wind?
  [8] *If not, what did you go out to see?*
  A man dressed in fine clothes?' NIV

Then Jesus explains that John is so great that he is referred to in scripture, and yet is a bit of a mystery, so a riddle is called for-

- Matthew 11:11 *'Truly I tell you, amongst those born to women*
  there has not risen anyone greater than John the baptist;
  yet whoever is least in the kingdom of heaven is greater than he.'

Such is the privileged position of the ordinary Christian.

****

---

192 'teachers of the law' - NIV
193 Matthew 12:27 and Luke 11:19 are similar.
194 Litotes

A curious thing happens in Matthew 13. First, Jesus tells the *parable of the sower* in verses 3 to 9.[195] Then, the disciples ask him why he teaches using parables all the time. Jesus explains-

- Matthew 13:11 ... *'Because the knowledge of the secrets of the kingdom of heaven has been given to you, but not to them ...'*

Jesus then quotes Isaiah 6, which explains that part of the function of parables is to condemn those who do not understand because of their hard, unbelieving, *hearts*. So we hope that, next, he will explain the parable of the sower to the disciples, because there were one or two details in the *parable* that we were perhaps not 100% clear about. He does so in verses 18 to 23, but perhaps we already suspect that he is playing with us a little, by delaying the explanation by seven verses!

Then, Jesus tells the *parable of the weeds* in verses 24 to 30. We expect him immediately to provide an explanation to the disciples, as we had hoped with the previous parable. This time, he doesn't!

Oh dear! Are we also amongst those who are hard-hearted and do not *understand*, for whom parables are a sign of God's condemnation?!

Jesus deliberately tells another parable, the *mustard seed*.

Then another, the *yeast*.

Then Matthew also inserts an explanation from Psalm 78:2-

- Matthew 13:35 *So was fulfilled what was spoken through the prophet:*
  'I will open my mouth in parables,
  I will utter things hidden since the creation of the world.'

Now we are really worried!

Only by the time we get to verse 36, does Jesus start to explain the *parable of the weeds*. Is this humour? If it is, it is mainly Jesus' humour, not Matthew's. It rather looks as if Jesus is teasing us, and perhaps with good reason: Is he enabling us to see that, to some extent, we are all unbelieving?

****

Jesus calls the Scribes and Pharisees *'blind guides'* at least three times.[196] In this example, he puts it humorously, presumably to highlight how ridiculous it would be to follow these false teachers-

---

195 Not 'the parable of the soils'; Jesus names it unambiguously in verse 18.
196 Matthew 15:14; 23:16; 23:24

- Matthew 15:14 *Leave them;*
  they are blind guides.
 If the blind lead the blind,
  both will fall into a pit.' NIV

And yet, if Jesus warns us, there must always be such danger. In Acts 20, the apostle Paul says farewell to the elders of the church in Ephesus. He uses no humour, but leaves them in no doubt that there will be *savage wolves* who will *distort the truth* and steal *disciples[197]*. We must ensure that both Paul's strong language, and Jesus' equally strong, and humorous, language, spur us to be on our guard for false teachers.

****

A more obvious pun than the one above in Matthew 4:18-20 is Jesus' renaming of Simon Peter[198]-

- Matthew 16:18 *And I tell you that you are Peter* [meaning rock],
  and on this rock I will build my church,
 and the gates of Hades will not overcome it.

This example is particularly interesting because Jesus not only makes a pun using the words Πέτρος *(Petros)* and πέτρα *(petra)*, but, by renaming Simon to *Peter*, Jesus also gives *Peter* a permanent reminder of his promise, *'on this rock I will build...'*, so that *Peter* could never really forget it.

****

The incident of the *two drachma temple tax* is only related to us by Matthew. This tax was instituted in Exodus 30:11-16 as a reminder that all God's people needed to be redeemed from the debt of sin and from slavery to sin. In Matthew 17:24, whether Jesus had to pay this tax or not was challenged indirectly via a question to Peter-

- Matthew 17:24 ...*'Doesn't your teacher pay the temple tax?'*
  [25] *'Yes, he does,' he replied.*

Of course, the one who was *born under the law[199], to redeem those under law,* was legally required to pay this tax. But Jesus explains how ridiculous it would be for the Redeemer to be redeemed in this way (17:25-26)! Jesus instructs Peter to go fishing once more, and to find a *four drachma coin* in a *fish's mouth.* The sudden doubling of the tax should alert us to humour being afoot!

---

197 Acts 20:29,30
198 Which is only recorded by Matthew.
199 Galatians 4:4-5

Using this coin would have the effect of complying with the law of Moses, but would also avoid unnecessary *offence* being caused (17:27). But why *four drachmas?*[200] The punchline is right at the end of the episode-

- Matthew 17:27 '… *Take it and give it to them for my tax and yours.*'

That final couple of words[201], "*and yours*", reveal that *Peter* himself had not paid his own *temple tax*! Probably, *Peter* was unable to pay. *Peter* too needed to be redeemed from his sin, not just pictorially by paying the *temple tax*, but in fact, by Jesus himself. By paying Peter's tax, Jesus modelled for us what he would later do by dying on the cross. This juxtapositioning of the Redeemer and the redeemed is beautiful humour by the Master of humour.

$$****$$

Jesus' parable of the unmerciful servant contains some behaviour that is at once shocking and amusing-

- Matthew 18:28 '*But when that servant went out, he found one of his fellow servants who owed him 100 silver coins* [i.e. 100 days' wages]. *He grabbed him and began to choke him. "Pay back what you owe me!" he demanded.*'

Our first reaction to such behaviour is probably shock: How can this man who has been shown such mercy treat another servant like that? But Jesus gives us a signal that this is only partly evil behaviour; it is also ridiculous. Jesus adds the seemingly unnecessary detail that the wicked servant *began to* throttle (ἔπνιγεν[202]) the other servant. So in addition to the juxtapositioning of mercy and ruthlessness, we have a verbal detail that adds some dark humour to the story. The humour paints a picture of the actual event in our minds, makes it more memorable, makes it more scary. We come away from the parable, hopefully, far less likely to be unforgiving to our brothers and sisters in Christ.

Something similar happens in Matthew 23 (Luke 11:52)-

- Matthew 23:13 '*Woe to you, teachers of the law and Pharisees, you hypocrites!*
  You shut the door of the kingdom of heaven in people's faces[203].' NIV

---

200 There may not have been a two drachma coin.
201 '*καὶ σοῦ.*' in the Greek.
202 The tense is the imperfect, and this is clearly an inceptive imperfect, hence the NIV's correct translation '*he began to choke…*'
203 '"Ἐμπροσθεν τῶν ἀνθρώπων'= before people, i.e. *in their faces*

That extra little phrase, *"in people's faces"*, helps us to feel the rudeness, the injustice, the ill-treatment of the ordinary people by the Pharisees, and helps to both understand and feel what Jesus' is saying.

The *'whited sepulchres'* imagery is very similar-

* Matthew 23:27 *'Woe to you, teachers of the law and Pharisees,*
    you hypocrites!
  You are like whitewashed tombs,
    which look beautiful on the outside
  but on the inside are full of the bones of the dead
    and everything unclean.' NIV

It conjures up a mental video of a man accidentally stepping into an unmarked grave and making himself ceremonially unclean. The people must have smiled at the ironic idea of the Pharisees *looking beautiful*. Then, the humour becomes an unmistakable insult aimed straight at those *beautiful* Pharisees. Jesus knows he is soon going to die and so does not pull any punches. The people have to know this at any cost. And the cost would be great.

****

Sometimes, Jesus' puns appear not to work very well. An example is-

* Matthew 23:24 *You blind guides!*
    You strain out a gnat but swallow a camel. NIV

Here Jesus uses a sharp insult to emphasise how ridiculous the Pharisees are being when they legalistically emphasise relatively unimportant laws at the expense of really important ones.

We look vainly for a pun in the pair of obvious words, *gnat* and *camel*. The Greek says κώνωπα and κάμηλον; that sounds like 'konopa' and kamelon'. At best that would seem to be some alliteration, i.e. where the first letters of the words are the same. Alliteration can be used to get onomatopoeic[204] effects in any language, e.g. "**r**ifles' **r**apid **r**attle". But we (reverently) feel that Jesus could have done better than that! And the truth is that he probably did.

Jesus may well have been speaking Aramaic, which was the common day to day language amongst the Jews at the time. In Aramaic, the words for *gnat* and *camel* sound much more similar[205], *"qalmâ"* and *"gamlâ"*, but it is impossible to be sure

---

204 Sounds that aurally suggest an action.
205 Gundry, R.H., *Matthew*, Eerdmans, 1994

exactly what Jesus did say, because there is no documentary evidence apart from the evangelists' Greek gospels themselves[206]. However, it could well be that Matthew could not reproduce the full Aramaic pun in Greek translation, and therefore settled for just an alliteration in Greek.

Nevertheless, Jesus' memorable puns enable us to think all the time about our priorities by recalling short, snappy proverbs.

****

Many other examples of Jesus' prolific humour are shared with Mark's or Luke's gospels, but one further thing has to be observed from Matthew's gospel. In chapter 9, Jairus[207] begs Jesus to heal his dead daughter, but then (to the mourners)-

- Matthew 9:24 [Jesus] *said, 'Go away. The girl is not dead but asleep.' But they started laughing[208] at him.*

It is obviously Jesus' statement that the noisy crowd were *laughing at.* Here is a blatant misuse of humour! But when God's people die, they are often said merely to be *asleep.* The mourners have no idea of either the depth or the power behind Jesus' statement, so they *laugh.*

The combination of Jairus' remarkable faith and Jesus' resurrecting power instantly restores life to the girl. But Jesus' mild rebuke, *'Go away',* followed by getting rid of the crowd is remarkable. Here was the Son of God, in the very process of giving life to one of his people, and yet the people's derision is hardly rebuked at all! What is going on here? Well surely we see not only Jesus' power in this incident, but also his voluntary humility. He came down to our level; he became one with us poor humans to such an extent that he was even willing to be insulted mid-miracle.

- Philippians 2:5 *In your relationships with one another, have the same mindset as Christ Jesus:*
  ⁶ who, being in very nature God, did not consider equality with God something to be used to his own advantage;[209] ⁷ rather, he made himself nothing by taking the very nature of a servant, being made in human likeness.

---

206 There are gospels in Aramaic, but it is obvious that these are translations of the Greek, not the other way around.

207 Mark 5:22,35; Luke 8:41,49-51

208 'κατεγέλων' '*began to laugh*' Unusually, the NIV has missed this inceptive imperfect.

209 The NIV 2011 would seem to be spot on, in verse 6.

8 And being found in appearance as a man,
he humbled himself... NIV

He became a joke for us. He showed us true humility.

8.2 Mark

Humour starts early in Mark's succinct gospel, when Jesus employs some sarcastic word-play to give two of his disciples a new, shared, name-

- Mark 3:17 ... James *son of Zebedee and his brother John*
  (to them he gave the name Boanerges, which means 'sons of thunder'...)

Whether they liked the name or not, they would certainly always now have a reminder of their besetting sin; *thundering*. That they share this title might imply that they tended to 'wind each other up'. If so, Jesus' playful wisdom is only magnified through the precise deployment of sarcastic humour in this case.

****

Mark 4:35-41, Matthew 8:23-27 and Luke 8:22-25 all describe the Lord Jesus, in his human exhaustion falling asleep. But in addition to Jesus' obvious exhaustion, they all note a huge contrast between Jesus, the man, asleep in the wildest storm, even though the boat was in danger of sinking, and the disciples, who panic and accuse Jesus-

- Mark 4:38 ... *'Teacher, don't you care if we drown?'*

The juxtapositioning of Jesus' peace and the disciples' panic makes an almost comic scene, and has all sorts of lessons to teach us about trusting in the Father's love. Mark's gospel has a major theme of faith versus unbelief that runs all the way through from chapter 2 to chapter 16.[210]

****

Mark 7:24-30 and Matthew 15:21-28 contain a mildly humorous story of how Jesus related to a Gentile woman[211]. At first, he refuses to heal her daughter and insults her-

- Mark 7:27 *'First let the children eat all they want,' he told her,*
  'for it is not right to take the children's bread and toss it to the dogs.' NIV

Now, where I lived, in Devon (UK), dogs are regarded as the highest form of life! But in Jesus' society, they were the lowest of the low, so Jesus uses the word *'dogs'* to

---

210 See for more: http://davidlegg.org.uk/what_is_mark_about.html accessed 06/07/2019.
211 Trueblood also finds humour earlier in Mark 7, verses 9-13; Matthew 15:5. The Pharisees are certainly being tricky.

refer to Gentiles. He is saying that he came first to save Abraham's descendants, and only after that to save Gentiles.

The woman replies-

- Mark 7:28 'Lord, ...*even the dogs under the table eat the children's crumbs.*'

So, Jesus immediately heals her daughter. It was not the woman's obvious wit that Jesus' responded to, but her humble faith. Even the original rebuttal in verse 27 was intended to draw out her faith. And it is fascinating to see how Jesus uses this crude form of humour, insult, to turn her desperation into faith. We can learn from such humble, persevering, prayer[212].

****

Mark 8:33 and Matthew 16:23 have *Peter* showing merely worldly concerns, not wanting Jesus to die, and for all the wrong reasons-

- Mark 8:33 *But when Jesus turned and looked at his disciples, he rebuked Peter. 'Get behind me, Satan!' he said. 'You do not have in mind the concerns of God, but merely human concerns.'* NIV

And with this stern rebuke, *Jesus* explains to *Peter* that he is actually doing *Satan's* work for him, because *Satan* is the one behind all *Peter's* worldly aspirations for both himself and his Lord. He certainly won't forget that in a hurry! What kind of insult is it? It is caricature delivered as hyperbole.

The huge irony, though, is that *Peter* had just correctly identified who *Jesus* was-

- Mark 8:29 *'But what about you?' he asked. 'Who do you say I am?'* *Peter answered, 'You are the Messiah.'* NIV

How the mighty have fallen! [213] When confronted with Jesus' true mission, Peter is also confronted with his own true self. Awkward, that.

Because Mark juxtapositioned the two passages, we not only see Jesus' humour, but also Mark's own humour.[214]

****

---

212 Even though the two parties were face to face, it was still prayer.

213 2 Samuel 1:19-27

214 Matthew does the same, but it is usually considered that Mark's gospel was written earlier. There are all sorts of source criticism theories out there, but they mainly belong to modernist, non-conservative, thought.

Mark 10:25, Matthew 19:24 and Luke 18:25 share this profound piece of hyperbole-

- Mark 10:25 [Jesus:] *It is easier for a camel*
  to go through the eye of a needle
than for someone who is rich
  to enter the kingdom of God.' NIV

Daft theories have been hatched to explain away Jesus' humour here, which I deliberately do not repeat here because they are made up. Jesus' point is simply this: It is impossible for a *rich* person to save himself. Jesus' rich imagery combined with that ironic point[215] cause us to give a sharp intake of breath. Especially if we are at all wealthy, because we are so powerfully influenced by money to the point of trusting in it for many things — food, shelter, health, entertainment, holidays, etc, if we are not very careful.

But then, Jesus mercifully releases the tension he has created-

- Mark 10:27 '*Jesus looked at them and said,*
  '*With man this is impossible,*
    but not with God;
  all things are possible with God.' NIV

Without Jesus' searching irony, we would never have examined our hearts, never have checked whether we are trusting in money, and not have checked whether we are relying upon anything but *God* himself for us to *enter the kingdom of heaven.*

****

Understandably, writers are afraid to see any kind of humour in Mark 15, Matthew 27 and Luke 23 because they record the crucifixion. And yet, if, as we have seen, humour is often reserved for the most serious occasions, would we not expect to find some in these Bible passages, very carefully, and very reverently, for we are treading on holy ground? [216]

Mark 15 has Jesus' enemies thinking they have triumphed over him. They mock him with the words-

- Mark 15:31 ...'*He saved others,' they said, 'but he cannot save himself!* NIV

The fact that they were mocking makes this a kind of humour, a grotesque kind, but definitely humour.

---

215 Ironic, because the rich are assumed to have been blessed by God.
216 Exodus 3:5

The fact that they were actually right, makes this irony into gospel irony! The only way that Jesus could *save other* people was by *not saving himself*. This is a profound, yet ironic, thought that goes right to the heart of the gospel.

In terms of Jesus' power and his identity, he could easily have *saved himself-*

- Matthew 26:53 '*Do you think I cannot call on my Father, and he will at once put at my disposal more than twelve legion of angels?*'

But in terms of Jesus' love, God's covenant plan, and divine justice, the enemies were correct; *he could not save himself*! I am amazed that this central gospel truth, in solemn scripture itself, is communicated to us using irony coming from mocking lips!

8.3 Luke

Only Luke preserves for us this, one of Jesus' many proverbs-

- Luke 5:39 *And no one after drinking old wine wants the new, for they say, "The old is better."* NIV

This piece of irony is intended to help us recognise ourselves. We need to recognise that we often prefer that *old* comfortable pair of slippers, for example, but the message of the proverb is the opposite. Jesus is saying that *the new* must come, and that *the new*, in this case, is his *new* covenant kingdom.

But we so easily insist on having (and I caricature mercilessly here) our old familiar pews, clunky Bible translations, traditional hymns, newer songs by that favourite writer, crusty old preachers, and musty church buildings, even though they might be well past their sell-by dates. The young insist on having loud contemporary music, sitting on the floor (or even standing all the time, in one church I know of), reading from a screen, and playing with smart-phones during sermons.

How we need wisdom to discern which of these are actually biblical norms, and which are simply our own cultural idols.[217]

****

---

217 For example, see Tim Keller's
http://www.fellowshipatlantic.com/editoruploads/files/Idols_of_the_Heart_by_Tim_Keller.pdf accessed 06/07/2019

Whereas Mark 5:25-26 records that Jesus is touched by a woman who has been bleeding for twelve years and…

- Mark 5:26 *She had suffered a great deal under the care of many doctors and had spent all she had, yet instead of getting better she grew worse.*

Luke identifies the same woman (Luke 8:42,43; Matthew 9:20) like this-

- Luke 8:43 *...bleeding for twelve years, but no one could heal her.*

In this way, we are instantly and humorously reminded that Luke was a *doctor!*[218] We are also reminded that he was a Gentile. All the previous writers have been Jewish. Whereas Matthew points out many Gentile-related facts in his Jewish gospel, Luke is an actual foreigner, and here he is contributing to divine scripture. Many Jews must have found that difficult to accept, but of course, Psalm 117 had been reminding them for around the last 1,000 years of God's purposes for us Gentiles-

- Psalm 117:1 *Praise the LORD, all you nations; extol him, all you peoples.*

We are also reminded that Luke was not an eye-witness to what he recorded in his gospel. Luke is the historian who travelled around and asked actual eye-witnesses and ear-witnesses what they saw and heard Jesus do and say-

- Luke 1:1 *Many have undertaken to draw up an account of the things that have been fulfilled[a] among us, ² just as they were handed down to us by those who from the first were eye witnesses and servants of the word. ³ With this in mind, since I myself have carefully investigated everything from the beginning, I too decided to write an orderly account for you, most excellent Theophilus, ⁴ so that you may know the certainty of the things you have been taught.*
  Footnote [a] Or been surely believed NIV

So it is not surprising that when Luke records Jesus' horticultural humour, it comes packaged differently from Matthew's account (7:34)-

- Luke 6:44 *… People do not pick figs from thorn-bushes, or grapes from thorns[219]. ⁴⁵ A good man brings good things out of the good stored up in his heart, and an evil man brings evil things out of the evil stored up in his heart. For the mouth speaks what the heart is full of.*

Where Matthew focused on the wolf-like danger of false teachers such as the Jewish Pharisees, Luke focuses on people's moral character, and on their heart-life.

****

---

218 Colossians 4:14
219 The NIV UK has briars, presumably an accidental Americanism

When Jesus pours scorn on the Pharisees in Matthew 23:25,26, Luke records this slightly differently-

- Matthew 23:25 *'Woe to you, teachers of the law and Pharisees, you hypocrites! You clean the outside of the cup and dish, but inside **they** are full of greed and self-indulgence.* [26] *Blind Pharisee! First clean the inside of the cup and dish, and then the outside also will be clean.'*

- Luke 11:39 *Then the Lord said to him, 'Now then, you Pharisees clean the outside of the cup and dish, but inside **you** are full of greed and wickedness.* [40] *You foolish people! Did not the one who made the outside make the inside also?* [41] *But now **as for what is inside you** — be generous to the poor, and everything will be clean for you.'*

Why the differences? Partly, Luke is recording what was said to one particular *Pharisee* in his own home (11:37). But also, Jesus makes the humour and the criticism more personal, on the occasion that Luke records for us. In both passages, Jesus is ridiculing the *Pharisees* for their overt hypocrisy, but in Luke's account, Jesus is really trying to help an individual *Pharisee* himself to repent.

****

Luke is the only evangelist to record Jesus' insult of Herod. Jesus has just been informed by the Pharisees that *Herod* Antipas *wants to kill* him-

- Luke 13:32 He replied, *'Go and tell that fox, "I will keep on driving out demons and healing people today and tomorrow, and on the third day I will reach my goal."*

The Lord is clearly not going to let crafty Herod *outfox* him in any way.[220]

****

In the Bible, vultures always have bad associations.[221] Luke 17:37 and Matthew 24:28 preserve for us a disparaging remark about the Roman forces gathering around the future ruins of Jerusalem, presumably in AD70-

- Luke 17:37 *'Where, Lord?'* [the disciples] *asked.*
  [Jesus] *replied, 'Where there is a dead body, there the vultures will gather.'*

---

220 NIC NT on Luke by Geldenhuis, reprint 1971, says Jesus was calling Herod *'a cunning, but weak, ruler'*
221 Leviticus 11:13; Deuteronomy 14:12; Job 30:17; Micah 1:16; Matthew 24:28; Luke 17:37

Jesus is certainly casting the surrounding Roman legions in an unfavourable rôle. Some have even suggested that the mention of *vultures* is actually an allusion to the Roman eagle. Whether that is the case or not, Jesus is certainly not complimenting the Romans for performing God's judgement on Jerusalem. Though the humour is dark, here is Jesus using humour as a vehicle for a prophetic prediction of the future.

****

Luke 6 contains the so-called 'sermon on the plain' (6:17—*level place* NIV) It closely parallels the sermon on the mount in verses 20-22, but the differences are interesting and instructive. The same paradoxes are there—*poor* versus great; *hungry* versus *satisfied; weeping* versus *laughing*, but there is also the juxtapositioning of a set of *woes* in verses 24-26.

Presumably Jesus wants to contrast the *poor* (20) with the *rich* (24), so he does not refer to the *poor* as the '*poor in spirit*' which could include *rich* people with a godly, *poor*, attitude. He simply contrasts the two groups of people with the single words, *poor* and *rich-*

- Luke 6:20 *Looking at his disciples, he said:*
  'Blessed are you who are **poor**,
      for yours is the kingdom of God.

- Matthew 5:3 *'Blessed are the* **poor** *in spirit,*
      for theirs is the kingdom of heaven.'

When Jesus adds the section of four *woes*, the teaching becomes sharper, more challenging, darker-

- Luke 6:24 *'But woe to you who are* **rich**,
      for you have already received your comfort.

Not only is the humour more pointed, but the juxtapositioning of *poor* and *rich* etc. make it obvious that these words cannot simply be assigned to wishy-washy spiritual categories, in order to water them down! No, he means us, be we *rich* or *poor*. There is no escaping this kind of hyperbole. One way or another, everyone is the target.

If you are *poor*, is it just through incompetence, 'bad luck', or laziness like Mr Micawber[222], or is it because you deliberately put first the *kingdom of God* and his righteousness, and thereby suffer through poverty?

---

222 David Copperfield, Charles Dickens, 1850.

Figure 14: Mr Micawber in Dickens' David Copperfield, a 1912 illustration by Fred Barnard wikipedia

If you are *rich*, is it because you are trusting in money like the rich fool? Or, are you *rich* like Abraham was, but in attitude you are actually *poor in spirit*?[223]

****

On Luke 7:31-35 (Matthew 11:16-19), Trueblood calls the unbelieving generation *'insatiable critics'*[224], but really they are just plain prejudiced-

- Luke 7:32 *They are like children sitting in the market-place and calling out to each other:*
  *'"We played the pipe for you,
      and you did not dance;
  we sang a dirge,
      and you did not cry."*
  [33] *For John the Baptist came neither eating bread nor drinking wine, and you say, "He has a demon."* [34] *The Son of Man came eating and*

---

223 Matthew 5:3
224 Only on p127 of op. cit.

drinking, and you say, "Here is a glutton and a drunkard, a friend of tax collectors and sinners." NIV

John and *Jesus* are polar opposites (in their view), but the people are happy with neither. Jesus employs a childish rhyme[225] to show them how perverse they are being.

Both Luke and Matthew then personify Jesus' verdict in slightly different ways-

- Matthew 11:19 '*... But wisdom is proved right by her deeds.*'
- Luke 7:35 '*But wisdom is proved right by all her children.*'

In both cases, *wisdom* is personified, presumably because the wise persons, *John* and *Jesus,* will both be vindicated! But here we have the Lord quoting and expounding a children's rhyme and then applying it.[226] The implication is that the unbelieving people are childish[227] — another insult.

****

Whilst I am not convinced that Luke 11:8 is really humorous[228], Luke 18:5 is a rather cynical joke at the expense of the judiciary-

- Luke 18:4 [The unjust judge:] "*Even though I don't fear God or care what people think, ⁵ yet because this widow keeps bothering me, I will see that she gets justice, so that she won't eventually come and attack me!*"'

As we saw with Luke 5:39, the actual meaning is the opposite of what is ironically portrayed: Our God is nothing like that judge, so we must keep on praying and never give up. Is Jesus saying that we must pester God? No, because that would be a plain contradiction of Matthew 6:7[229]. Jesus is definitely being humorous here, and when there is humour, we must be prepared for the meaning of a saying to be non-literal.

The argument is from the lesser to the greater by means of some irony: If the unjust man caved in, how much more readily will your completely just, heavenly Father, listen? So keep praying until he does.

****

Jesus gives us an unsettling pair of parables in Luke 14 to teach us to be ready for the cost of following him. The gist is that we ourselves will be the butt of the joke if we are unprepared for what discipleship means-

---

225 Akin to '*Mary, Mary, quite contrary*'.
226 This is a similar practice to that of Paul on Mars Hill, where he quotes Epimenides and Aratus, who were both Greek philosophers. Acts 17:28
227 Not to be confused with *childlike.* Luke 18:17
228 As Trueblood is, p127, '*Successful Pestering*'
229 '*... they think they will be heard because of their many words.*' NIV

- Luke 14:29 *For if you lay the foundation and are not able to finish it, everyone who sees it will ridicule you, [30] saying, "This person began to build and wasn't able to finish."* NIV

- 14:31 *'Or suppose a king is about to go to war against another king. Won't he first sit down and consider whether he is able with ten thousand men to oppose the one coming against him with twenty thousand?'* NIV

The humour is not so much in how Jesus' initially delivers the wisdom, but in how we might look and feel if we are later caught out. Following Jesus is serious, so humour is deployed to make sure we know Jesus is not joking!

****

Finally, in Luke, we see Jesus himself being *mocked* and *beaten*, becoming the butt of the joke, enduring scorn and other nasty forms of humour-

- Luke 22:63 *The men who were guarding Jesus began mocking and beating him. [64] They blindfolded him and demanded, 'Prophesy! Who hit you?' [65] And they said many other insulting things to him.* NIV

The soldiers think it is just a practical joke, but it is Jesus being humiliated for us. This kind of humour should make us soberly grateful for all that he endured on our behalf. We were stupid so he took the *mocking*. We were evil, so he took the *beating*. We spent our lives *blind* to grace, but he was the one *blindfolded*. He was *insulted* so that we may one day share in his glory.[230] It is all so wrong, so humbling, but nevertheless an example of humour.

8.4 John

John's gospel stands in stark contrast to the synoptic gospels[231] by containing almost no humour. There a little in the last paragraph, almost as if John finally relaxes and lightens up, having finished his magnum opus, John's Gospel. Before that, there is this mildly amusing exchange-

- John 1:45 *Philip found Nathanael and told him, 'We have found the one Moses wrote about in the Law, and about whom the prophets also wrote — Jesus of Nazareth, the son of Joseph.'*

  [46] *'Nazareth! Can anything good come from there?' Nathanael asked.* NIV

---

230 1 Peter 5:1
231 Matthew, Mark and Luke are considered to have been written from similar viewpoints.

Nazareth clearly has a poor or even comical association in *Nathanael's* mind. This may have come from *the prophets*, as shown by Matthew-

- John 1:23 … *and he went and lived in a town called Nazareth. So was fulfilled what was said through the prophets, that he would be called a Nazarene*[232]. NIV

But the problem is, which *prophets*? There were three types of *prophet*: the writers of scripture e.g. Moses; the doing-*prophets* e.g. Elijah; and the speaking-*prophets* e.g. Anna in Luke 2:36. The *prophets* referred to by John are clearly not the writers of scripture, or it would be easy to find a cross-reference for Matthew 2:23. Nor are they likely to be the doing-*prophets* such as Elijah, because, in any case, most of what they did and said would only be known about through scripture. So it seems likely that the predictions that the Messiah would *come from Nazareth* and be *called a Nazarene* may have come from one of the speaking *prophets*. There seem to have been many of these as is shown by 1 Samuel 10, 2 Kings 2 and Luke 2:36.

Nazareth also seems to have acquired its own negative reputation in at least *Nathanael's* mind. Perhaps John 1:46 was a bit like saying, "Can anything good come out of Bognor?" And perhaps we will never know.

But it is certainly true to say that Jesus' origins were obscured by having been brought up in *Nazareth* rather than in Bethlehem, the town of King David[233]. His home town seems to have been a part of his voluntary humiliation on behalf of the poor and despised that he came to save. John points this out for us by quoting *Nathanael's* mildly insulting remark about *Nazareth* in John 1:46. Insult is a common class of humour, even in the Bible.

But generally, John evades opportunities for humour. In John 1:42, John carefully leaves out the well-known pun on Simon Peter's new name (Cf. Matthew 16:18). Jesus' justification for clearing out the temple is a potential riddle-

- John 2:19 '*Destroy this temple*[234], *and I will raise it again in three days.*' NIV

But this is about Jesus' death and resurrection, so John gives no textual clues that this might be humour.

In John 3:4, Nicodemus thinks Jesus is joking, but he isn't.

---

232 There does not seem to be any direct association between being a *Nazarene* from *Nazareth* and the *Nazirite vows* in Numbers 6.
233 Matthew 2:5-8
234 Jesus is the fulfilment of everything that the temple merely typified.

Nor does there seem to be any actual humour in Jesus' instruction to the immoral woman, in John 4, to go and get her non-existent husband; he is simply putting a finger on her sin. And so on[235].

Only at the very end of his gospel, does John seem to allow himself a little levity-

- John 21:25 *Jesus did many other things as well. If every one of them were written down, I suppose that even the whole world would not have room for the books that would be written.* NIV

John conjures up an image in our minds of a *world* entirely populated by *books* about *Jesus*, that overflows because there is still not enough room. It is a delightful image.

After John has finished recounting his largely eye-witness, traumatic, account of everything Jesus suffered, and had often been omitted for valid reasons by the synoptic writers, he remembers that the gospel is good news! He lifts our moods with the last verse of his own gospel by combining subtle praise of *Jesus* with a little joke about how important he is, as measured by the number of books that could be written about him![236]

8. Humour in Acts

Acts is the closest thing that the New Testament has to a history book, and is filled with narrative, so we would expect it to be fertile soil for growing biblical humour. Indeed, David Peters says that he considers Luke to be the most humorous of all the biblical writers.[237]

What is Acts about? It is about how Acts 1:8 is fulfilled — the gospel goes from *Jerusalem*, to *Samaria* and to the *ends of the earth*. It is about how the gospel came to Europe, how it got all the way to Rome. And as Luke put pen to papyrus, he was probably many miles away from Israel. So, it must have been with a wry grin on his face that he wrote about how the disciples asked Jesus-

- Acts 1:6 ... '*Lord, are you at this time going to restore the kingdom to Israel?*' NIV

The level of Jonah-like nationalism exuded by this question is palpable. As Calvin wrote-

---

235 See John 6:70; 8:58; 9:30; 11:50; 12:19; 19:3; 19:5.
236 And here we are, still doing it!
237 *The Many Faces of Biblical Humor*(sic), David A. Peters, Hamilton Books, 2008

- *'There are as many errors in this question as words.'*[238]

****

But most of the humour in Acts is not just a matter of how Luke narrated. Some comes from the uncomprehending Jews on the day of Pentecost-

- Acts 2:13 *Some, however, made fun of them and said,*
    "They have had too much wine." NIV

Other humour comes from the power of the Holy Spirit who enabled the early church to behave with such *boldness*. In Acts 4:3, the apostles have already preached the good news with great *boldness*, to the extent that they have been arrested. They are then threatened, and then threatened a bit more (4:21), so what do they do? They go straight back to the infant church and ask the *Lord* Jesus[239] for even more *boldness*!

- Acts 4:29 *Now, Lord, consider their threats*
    and enable your servants to speak your word with great boldness. NIV

As Luke recalls what his eye-witnesses told him about the early days, he replays them with wit and irony. However, with the murder of Stephen, the mood soon changes.

But even with the morbid historical background to subsequent events in Acts, some humour is still allowed. In Acts 9, Ananias is given a job to do: Baptise Saul, the arch persecutor of the church. Ananias says the equivalent of, *"You canNOT be SERIOUS!"* to *the Lord* Jesus. At this, *the Lord* seems to give him a hard kick in the direction of *Straight Street*, where Saul is praying-

- Acts 9:15 *But the Lord said to Ananias, 'Go! This man is my chosen instrument to proclaim my name to the Gentiles and their kings and to the people of Israel.* NIV

At this, we wonder how willing we would be to rush off and baptise a newly converted Richard Dawkins, for example! Maybe we need some of that *boldness* that the disciples were praying for in Acts 4?

****

In terms of humour in Acts, the absolute peach has to be when the disciples are praying for the release of *Peter* from prison. They do not realise it yet, but an *angel* has already freed him, and he is *knocking on the door* of the house where they are having their intense prayer meeting-

- Acts 12:13 *Peter knocked at the outer entrance, and a servant named Rhoda came to answer the door. [14] When she recognised Peter's voice, she was so overjoyed*

---

238 Calvin, Complete Works, Vol. 36 Part I Acts 1:6-8. Available on-line.
239 'The Lord' often seems to mean specifically Jesus in Acts.

she ran back without opening it and exclaimed, 'Peter is at the door!'
NIV

And it is not just Rhoda who is worthy of our amusement, they were all at it-

- Acts 12:15 *'You're out of your mind,' they told her.*
  When she kept insisting that it was so, they said, 'It must be his angel.' NIV

In fact, they were so spiritually-minded that they had no trouble believing in *angels*. Believing that God had answered their prayers, however, was another completely different matter. We would never do something like that nowadays.

****

By Acts 10, it is becoming really clear that Gentiles can become Christians too. God, in his providence, arranges for *Simon Peter* to stay with another *Simon, Simon the Tanner* at the seaside (10:6). It sounds nice, doesn't it? A room with a view by the sea. But actually it was probably a room with a 'phew!'. Simon's tanning business would have filled the house with the smell of dead animals and their skins. The whole idea of tanning them was to stop them festering and make them into wearable pieces of leather etc.

Now Peter was feeling very Jewish, and abhorred anything unclean, especially those dirty Gentiles. Furthermore, the law explicitly forbade any encounters with dead things. But the Lord is about to give him a vision of a net full of forbidden animals to kill and eat (10:13). It is hard to miss the divine humour of Peter staying in a house smelling of dead animals to prepare him for accepting Gentiles as Christians, and as equals (for that is the implication of *Simon* the Tanner and *Simon* Peter sharing a name, as Luke tells it).

And we too, should be on the look-out for when God is preparing us in some way to serve him better. If you are reading this on holiday beside the sea, there could be a good reason for it…

Later, the gospel has made it all the way to Athens. The apostle Paul is seriously upset to find the city totally idol-ridden.[240] He thinks something like, "How am I ever to explain to these idolaters that idols are the very antipathy of the true *God*?" Then the true *God* gives him an idea in the

---

240 Strictly 'κατε-ίδωλον'

form of some terribly ironic, providential, humour, and his sermon begins to take shape-

- Acts 17:23 *'For as I walked around and looked carefully at your objects of worship, I even found an altar with this inscription: to an unknown god. So you are ignorant of the very thing you worship — and this is what I am going to proclaim to you.'* NIV

Paul quotes no scripture whatsoever, just a couple of pagan poets. With a recent divine providence of that order of magnitude, how was it that he preached such an unbiblical sermon, you ask?

We are so used to biblical exposition that we have difficulty coping with Paul's sermon to these biblically illiterate Atheneans.

But on closer inspection, we find that his sermon is not actually unbiblical; it is just very light on exact biblical quotations. In fact, many of the verses assert biblical truth, e.g. 17:24-27;30-31. Paul is not doing what might have suited him; he is doing what suits them. As he puts it in I Corinthians-

- 1 Corinthians 9:21 *To those not having the law I became like one not having the law ..., so as to win those not having the law.* ²²*... I have become all things to all people so that by all possible means I might save some.* NIV

This is an important lesson that *Simon* Peter too needed to learn as he lay on his bed trying to ignore the smell of dead animal at the home of *Simon* the tanner. It is also one that we need to learn as we sit in the comfort of our church buildings with everything arranged to suit us, as we advance in years. We need to think about how to suit those perishing outside.

****

Just when we thought the world of paganism had exhausted its ability to deliver side-achingly funny humour, there is a riot in Ephesus. The apostle Paul, it seems, has impacted the idol trade, so a riot ensues. The rioters are clearly motivated by money, but *Demetrius the silversmith* justifies the riot using devoutly spiritual reasoning!-

- Acts 19:27 *There is danger not only that our trade will lose its good name, but also that the temple of the great goddess Artemis will be discredited; and the goddess herself, who is worshipped throughout the province of Asia and the world, will be robbed of her divine majesty.'* NIV

When the crowd twigs that apostle Paul is a non-pagan-

- Acts 19:34 ... *they all shouted in unison for about two hours:* *'Great is Artemis of the Ephesians!'* NIV

Finally, the *city clerk* defuses the riot by asserting *Artemis'* sovereignty and the rioters' orthodoxy-

- Acts 19:35 *'Fellow Ephesians, doesn't all the world know that the city of Ephesus is the guardian of the temple of the great Artemis and of her image, which fell from heaven? 36 Therefore, since these facts are undeniable, you ought to calm down and not do anything rash.'* NIV

The writer, Luke, makes no comment on all this; he just records it as reported, and waits for the reader to pick himself up off the floor, before continuing with the next chapter. Such humour is reminiscent of Elijah and the priests of Baal in 1 Kings 18:26-29; it laughs scornfully at paganism, and does as much to build our faith in the true God, as the miracles that Paul had previously done in Ephesus (19:11); such is the power of humour.

****

The incident of Eutychus falling asleep while Paul preached *'on and on'* (NIV) in Acts 20:9 appeals to our 21st Century sense of humour. There are no clues in the text, so one suspects that the incident was not intended to be funny by Luke. But preaching has had such a bad name in the last fifty years, that we find Eutychus' somnolence amusing. This is a pity.

****

Acts 23:12-24, however, is left hanging in such an obviously humorous way that there is no doubt that we are intended to laugh at the enemies of the apostle *Paul* who had previously committed themselves to fast until they *killed* him! (23:12)-

- Acts 23:12 *The next morning some Jews formed a conspiracy and bound themselves with an oath not to eat or drink until they had killed Paul.*

We laugh with God's sovereignty that arranges for Paul to hear of the plot via his nephew (23:16).

We laugh at the enemies of the gospel, who made an oath reminiscent of Jephthah's vow[241]. The way that Luke just leaves them fasting, with absolutely no further comment, has the effect of emphasising the humour in a very rewarding way for the reader.

---

241 Judges 11:30ff

****

A final piece of humour worth noticing is in[242] Acts 26-

- Acts 26:14 *"Saul, Saul, why do you persecute me?*
  It is hard for you to kick against the goads."

Paul himself is giving his testimony to *King Agrippa*, but the words themselves were spoken by Jesus (26:15). The Lord gives *Saul* a very memorable image of an animal resisting the prodding of a keeper by kicking the very stick[243] being used to steer it. The ridiculousness of a human willingly doing something so painful highlights Paul's foolishness prior to his conversion. He was resisting Jesus; he was persecuting Jesus' church. It is instructive to us that the subject of persecution is alluded to using Jesus' own humour.

9. Humour in Paul's Letters

As we turn from Acts, where Luke narrates Paul's progress towards Rome in an often witty and humorous way, we straight away bump into Paul's own letters. It has to be conceded that Paul rarely made use of humour.

9.1 Romans

The theme of Romans is *righteousness* — definitely not a joking matter, but Paul does use darker forms of humour to make some of his points-

- Romans 2:21 ... *you, then, who teach others, do you not teach yourself?* NIV

That is definitely sarcasm. Paul uses it to criticise the Judaisers who are trying to take the moral high ground, and get the Roman Christians to be *circumcised.*

In Romans 4, Paul plays a little trick on his readers-

- Romans 4:9 ... *Abraham's faith was credited to him as righteousness.* [10]
  Under what circumstances was it credited?
  Was it after he was circumcised, or before?
  It was not after, but before! NIV

The reader is invited to think that Abraham was counted as *righteous* because he was *circumcised.* But Paul then ambushes the misled reader by showing that it was his

---

242 Ancient manuscripts have a habit of growing over time, as helpful scribes add additional information, sometimes retrieved from elsewhere in scripture, e.g. Acts 9:5 in the KJV/AV. It is probable that the *kicking against the pricks* verse only occurred in Acts 26:14 in the original manuscript.
243 A *goad* is a sharpened stick.

faith that must have been the essential ingredient, because Abraham was *circumcised after* he became legally *righteous*!

In Romans 16, Paul urges his readers to watch out for divisive false teachers-

- Romans 16:18 *For such people are not serving our Lord Christ, but their own appetites. By smooth talk and flattery they deceive the minds of naïve people.* NIV

The mechanism he uses is to label his readers *naïve* should they ever fall for the schemes of the Judaisers. He is appealing to their future feelings of discomfort and humiliation, should they be taken in.

9.2 I Corinthians

Paul's letters to the Corinthians are full of figures of speech, exclamations, rhetorical questions and other speaking devices. These make one wonder if reading the letter would be a similar experience to hearing the apostle preach?

Paul is addressing the problem of the church's sectarian pride and associated conflicts. So, he exaggerates their spiritual wealth and ironically contrasts that with his own apparent poverty-

- 1 Corinthians 4:8 *Already you have all you want! Already you have become rich! You have begun to reign —and that without us! How I wish that you really had begun to reign so that we also might reign with you!* NIV

He then contrasts his own approach to ministry with their own arrogant attitudes-

- 1 Corinthians 4:10 *We are fools for Christ, but you are so wise in Christ! We are weak, but you are strong! You are honoured, we are dishonoured!* [11] *To this very hour we go hungry and thirsty, we are in rags, we are brutally treated, we are homeless.* [12] *We work hard with our own hands. When we are cursed, we bless; when we are persecuted, we endure it;* [13] *when we are slandered, we answer kindly. We have become the scum of the earth, the rubbish*[244] *of the world — right up to this moment.*

This is preposterous incongruity but, at the same time, irony. He wants to show them two extreme opposites: his attitude and theirs. And yet, he does

---

244 The NIV (UK) has an Americanism here: *garbage.*

not want to *shame* them (4:14) but to *warn* them. Most of us would find it difficult to be so purely motivated and humorous without lapsing into scorn and derision. But later, a godly incidence of *scorn* is perhaps demonstrated-

- 1 Corinthians 6:3 *Do you not know that we will judge angels? How much more the things of this life! ⁴ Therefore, if you have disputes about such matters, do you ask for a ruling from those whose way of life is scorned in the church?*[245] NIV

Apparently some Christians had gone to law against other Christians, thus asking the *scorned* unbeliever to pronounce judgement upon a Christian. And this time, he does want them to be ashamed-

- 1 Corinthians 6:5 *I say this to shame you. Is it possible that there is nobody among you wise enough to judge a dispute between believers?* NIV

The question above is quite sarcastic, but makes the point that surely some-one in the church is able to mediate in the dispute.

The apostle Paul then describes fully co-operative 'body ministry' in the local church. But he resorts to caricature and ridicule in order to describe the Corinthians' abject failure to do it-

- 1 Corinthians 12:21 *The eye cannot say to the hand, 'I don't need you!'*
  And the head cannot say to the feet, 'I don't need you!' NIV

In chapter 13, he continues to ridicule their divisions-

- 1 Corinthians 13:1 *If I speak in the languages of men or of angels, but do not have love, I am only a resounding gong or a clanging cymbal.* NIV

He likens them to noisy but useless percussion. But it is in chapter 14 that he chooses extreme irony to rebuke their unbridled speaking in unlearned languages[246]-

- 1 Corinthians 14:21 *In the Law it is written:*
  'With other tongues
      and through the lips of foreigners
  I will speak to this people, ... [Isaiah 28:11] NIV

What is Paul doing here? He is saying that if they keep blathering away in untranslated languages at church, it is just as if God's people are in exile again, as per the quotation from Isaiah. It is a sign of God's judgement on them when they have to listen to *foreigners* speaking!

---

245 Obviously, if the NIV 1984 was correct in 6:4, the humour would be different: 6:4 ... *appoint as judges even men of little account in the church!*
246 Traditionally, *tongues*

Just when we feel he has beaten them up enough, he pours scorn on their gross ignorance-

- 1 Corinthians 15:35 *But someone will ask,*
  'How are the dead raised?
  With what kind of body will they come?'
  ^{36} *How foolish!* NIV

Well that was a straightforward insult, presumably well-deserved, and succinctly delivered! Most of the humour in I Corinthians is cutting, targeted, specific and emotive. We wonder what kind of congregation they were? How could they need such aggressive humour from Paul? Then we wonder why the Lord has allowed this letter to be preserved so that we can read it too. Humbling.

9.3 II Corinthians

II Corinthians is dominated by Paul pretending to be a boastful fool in order to make the point that, actually, he is a true apostle, deserves their acceptance, respect and obedience. In chapter 10, he starts by caricaturing his own reputation that he has heard he has with them-

- 2 Corinthians 10:1 I, *Paul, who am 'timid' when face to face with you,*
  but 'bold' towards you when away! NIV

He hopes that they will recognise their own poor attitudes to their apostle, and repent. The real *'foolishness'* starts in chapter 11, where he ladles on the sarcasm-

- 2 Corinthians 11:1 *I hope you will put up with me in a little foolishness.*
  Yes, please put up with me! ^{2} *I am jealous for you with a godly jealousy.*
  I promised you to one husband, to Christ... NIV

See also 2 Corinthians 11:16,17,19; 12:6,11. Paul is expressing marital jealousy, except that he is not their *husband*: *Christ* is! He is prepared to make a complete fool of himself if only he can persuade them to adopt godly attitudes to himself and to his ministry, thereby saving themselves from the dangers of being misled by some so-called *'super-apostles'*-

- 2 Corinthians 12:11 *I have made a fool of myself, but you drove me to it.*
  I ought to have been commended by you, for I am not in the least
  inferior to the 'super-apostles', even though I am nothing. NIV

He uses sarcasm to defend his own relationship with them-

- 2 Corinthians 12:13 *How were you inferior to the other churches, except that I was never a burden to you? Forgive me this wrong!* NIV

- 2 Corinthians 12:16 ... *Yet, crafty fellow that I am, I caught you by trickery!* NIV

We find II Corinthians 11 and 12 difficult to read. But the reason for this is that we are taking him too prosaically. He is pouring on the sarcasm, and we are just not used to that in scripture; we still consider sarcasm to be *the lowest form of wit.*[247] In the hands of Paul, sarcasm is a devastatingly serious weapon. We, however, need to be very careful how we use the circular saw of sarcasm.

9.4 Galatians

In Galatians, Paul uses every tactic that he can muster in order to bring the Galatians to their senses[248], including humour. He appeals to the ridiculous-

- Galatians 2:17 '*But if, in seeking to be justified in Christ, we Jews find ourselves also among the sinners, doesn't that mean that Christ promotes sin? Absolutely not!* NIV

He insults them-

- Galatians 3:1 *You foolish Galatians! Who has bewitched you?* NIV

He points out their contradictory reasoning-

- Galatians 3:21 *Is the law, therefore, opposed to the promises of God? Absolutely not!* NIV

And resorts to the gothic-

- Galatians 5:12 *As for those agitators, I wish they would go the whole way and emasculate themselves!* NIV

People have often struggled to understand 5:12. Did Paul really mean that? How unloving! But the real reason he writes something so extreme is not a lack of love, it is a surfeit of love. So, he employs the gothic, sarcastic, hyperbole to exaggerate circumcision, to show it for the horror it really is.

And finally, he displays his own desperation[249]-

- Galatians 6:11 *See what large letters I use as I write to you with my own hand!* NIV

---

247 Supposedly Oscar Wilde: *sarcasm — the highest form of intelligence but the lowest form of wit*
248 Even double-cursing: 1:8-9
249 Paul probably wrote the end of the letter himself, rather using an amanuensis, in order to authenticate the document. See 1 Corinthians 16:21; Colossians 4:18; 2 Thessalonians 3:17; Philemon 19;

If these foolish Galatians show contempt for God and so allow themselves to be circumcised, they will *sow* in legalism what they later *reap* in destruction!

- Galatians 6:7 *Do not be deceived: God cannot be mocked. A man reaps what he sows.* NIV

Once again, we notice that laughing with God is good, but laughing at him, *mocking* him by trying to *deceive* him, is not.

9.5 Ephesians

Although Paul does not seem to employ humour in Ephesians, he does teach about it-

- Ephesians 5:4 *Nor should there be obscenity, foolish talk or coarse joking, which are out of place, but rather thanksgiving.* NIV

This rather begs the question, "What was that *joking* in Galatians 5:12?"[250] It was certainly *coarse*, even crude, but not mere *joking*. In Ephesians, perhaps Paul is thinking of ribaldry? Scripture makes full use of humour for good purposes, but not for mere entertainment.

We too need to be careful how we use our tongues, and be most careful when there is already levity in the air.[251]

9.6 Philippians

Philippians also seems to be very light in humour. However, Paul does juxtapose the concepts of *love, joy* and conflict when he addresses two warring women-

- Philippians 4:1 *Therefore, my brothers and sisters, you whom I love and long for, my joy and crown, stand firm in the Lord in this way, dear friends!*
  2 I plead with Euodia and I plead with Syntyche to be of the same mind in the Lord. NIV

His textual consistency, using words like *love* and *joy* contradicts *Euodia's and Syntyche's* inter-personal conflict. They are *sisters*[252] and *dear friends*[253], and so should behave as such.

---

250 See the previous section on Galatians 5:12.
251 James 3:2
252 *Brothers and sisters* is ἀδελφοί.
253 *Dear friends* is ἀγαπητοί = loved ones.

Paul then fits in a quick insult to the circumcising Judaisers-

- Philippians 3:2 *Watch out for those dogs, those evildoers, those mutilators of the flesh.*

Just in case they hadn't got it the first time[254], a sarcastic reminder should help keep the Philippian *brothers and sisters* safe! We should never despise the preacher who revisits something familiar, but should use it as an opportunity for being warned, and for spiritual safety.

Just near the end of the letter, is Paul perhaps enjoying a little gospel triumph?-

- Philippians 4:22 *All God's people here send you greetings,
  especially those who belong to Caesar's household.* NIV

I hope so.

9.7 Colossians

Paul's shorter letters usually[255] make minimal use of humour, but it is still present-

- Colossians 2:20 *Since you died with Christ to the elemental spiritual forces of this world, why, as though you still belonged to the world, do you submit to its rules: [21] 'Do not handle! Do not taste! Do not touch!'?*

Here, Paul caricatures the rules of worldly religion as being composed of short, sharp, negatives. Such asceticism is superficial and does nothing to help the Christian.

9.8 I and II Thessalonians

I and II Thessalonians are a very sunny pair of letters, almost entirely without criticism of the church. They also seem to be devoid of humour! Does this observation shine a light on Paul's use of humour? Is humour used mainly as a form of criticism? It would seem so.

In 1 Thessalonians 2:3 he denies any *trickery* on his part.

In 2 Thessalonians 1:4 he *boasts*, but not in the way that he did in II Corinthians; this is sober boasting about the Thessalonians' *perseverance* and *faith*.

He allows himself a little triumph and delight at the thought of an Antichrist being destroyed-

---

254 Philippians 3:1
255 But not Philemon

- 2 Thessalonians 2:8 *And then the lawless one will be revealed, whom the Lord Jesus will overthrow with the breath of his mouth and destroy by the splendour of his coming.* NIV

But this is not really humour. Humour is not always needed, we discover. In fact, we have to wait almost to the end of this pair of letters to trip over a little word play-

- 2 Thessalonians 3:11 *We hear that some among you are idle and disruptive.*
  *They are not **busy**; they are **busybodies**.* NIV

This comes across well in English translation[256] and fits in well with the positive tone of both letters.

9.9 I and II Timothy

I and II Timothy are humour-free, and lead up to 2 Timothy 4, where Paul is expecting to die soon-

- 2 Timothy 4:6 *For I am already being poured out like a drink offering, and the time for my departure is near.* NIV

But just before that, he extricates a smidgen of levity to describe people in the near future who only want sermons that they already agree with-

- 2 Timothy 4:3 ... *they will gather round them a great number of teachers*
  to say what their itching ears want to hear. NIV

Heaven forbid that we should ever fall into such a category! Brothers and sisters, we must make sure that we regularly hear preaching that disagrees with us, challenges us, rebukes us, strengthens us, and motivates us. That kind of *itch* is a *hungering and thirsting for righteousness.*[257]

9.10 Titus

Paul's letter to Titus contains a sarcastic quote from Epimenides of Crete, a philosopher-poet-

- Titus 1:12 *One of Crete's own prophets has said it: 'Cretans are always liars, evil brutes, lazy gluttons.'* [Epimenides] *[13] This saying is true.*

---

256 Greek: 'μηδὲν ἐργαζομένους ἀλλὰ περιεργαζομένους'
257 Matthew 5:6

People wonder how the Bible can contain such stereotyping. Whilst the stereotyping of people can be a dangerous thing, avoiding it altogether is surely just political correctness. The apostle Paul found it useful to commandeer a popular, well-known, stereotype, and to apply it to certain false teachers. The insulting stereotype increased the 'punch' of Paul's warning and therefore was only a good thing[258].

Unlike the king in Jeremiah 36:23, who used his own wisdom to cut scripture with a literal knife, we must ensure that we allow scripture to apply its surgical *sword* to us-

- Hebrews 4:12 *For the word of God is alive and active. Sharper than any double-edged sword, it penetrates even to dividing soul and spirit, joints and marrow; it judges the thoughts and attitudes of the heart. ¹³ Nothing in all creation is hidden from God's sight. Everything is uncovered and laid bare before the eyes of him to whom we must give account.* NIV

9.11 Philemon

Paul's letter to *Philemon* is humorous as a whole, and therefore very serious. It is noticeable that, before he risks any humour, Paul gives the warmest imaginable greetings to *Philemon* and his family in verses 1 to 7. But then, the rest of the letter contains a very tongue-in cheek argument as to why *Philemon* should forgive *Onesimus*, an escaped slave who has become a Christian-

- 11 *Formerly he was* **useless** *to you, but now he has become* **useful** *both* **to you** *and* **to me***.*

The pun[259] works well in English, as does the symmetry of *'to you'* and *'to me'*, enhancing the irony. Then there is a lovely, disingenuous, joke-

- 17 *So if you consider me a partner,*
    welcome him as you would welcome me.
    ¹⁸ If he has done you any wrong or owes you anything,
    charge it to me. NIV

After the glowing commendation in verses 4 to 7, Paul's *'if you consider me a partner'* in verse 17 is surely an almost 'English' piece of understatement, or litotes. The notion that *Philemon* would bill Paul for any costs incurred (verse 18) is laughable!

But then Paul seems to have a tiny doubt that *Philemon* will take his offer humorously, and adds-

---

258 It is also more complex than this, because Epimenides' statement is an example of a 'liar paradox'.
259 ἄχρηστον ... εὔχρηστον

- 19 ... *I will pay it back — not to mention that you owe me your very self.* NIV

And, mere seconds after the letter has been read by Philemon, we fully expect *Onesimus* to pop out from behind a pillar and greet his *brother* (verse 16), *Philemon*!

10. Humour in the Other Letters

10.1 Hebrews

Nowadays, few think that Hebrews was written by the apostle Paul, apart from maybe the last six verses, 13:20-25.[260] So, we might expect a new style of humour that is obviously not Pauline, but actually, there is very little humour at all.

The early chapters are exclusively about the supremacy of Christ in every way, but by the time we arrive at chapter 5, the author is ready for a rebuke-

- Hebrews 5:12 *In fact, though by this time you ought to be teachers, you need someone to teach you the elementary truths of God's word all over again.*
  You need milk, not solid food! NIV

The frustrated humour is clearly an insult, but one intended to shame the Hebrew Christians. Considering the seriousness of the warnings in Hebrews about not falling away, this is quite a mild piece of humour.

One wonders whether the author's description of Abraham as nearly *dead* was originally intended as humorous-

- Hebrews 11:12 *And so from this one man, and he as good as dead, came descendants as numerous as the stars in the sky and as countless as the sand on the seashore.* NIV

Modern Western sensibilities about old age aside, this is certainly hyperbole, but more in amazement at God's power than in jest.

So, although Hebrews is quite a large letter, it contains very little humour. What there is does not stand out as being obviously Pauline. However, it does challenge us not to be theological milksops. We must not be afraid of theology books, and should give high priority to reading and understanding the Bible, if we are to avoid being like spiritual babies (5:12)!

---

260 See Our Brother Timothy by John D. Legg
  http://davidlegg.org.uk/our_brother_timothy.html accessed 13/07/2019

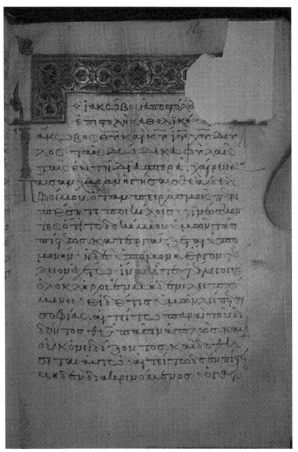

*Figure 15: The first page of James,
Minuscule 85 (Gregory-Aland) 12th Century,
public domain*

10.2 James

Perhaps more than any other letter, James has Christlike content. He was, after all, Jesus' biological brother.[261] There are many short parables and proverbs. James 1 contains an obvious riddle-

- James 1:9 *Believers in **humble** circumstances ought to take pride in their **high** position.* NIV

Later, there is a straightforward command followed by quite a funny parable-

- James 1:22 *Do not merely listen to the word, and so deceive yourselves. Do what it says.*

---
261 The other James was the son of Zebedee. Matthew 4:21; 10:2; 20:20; 27:56

²³ Anyone who listens to the word but does not do what it says is like someone who looks at his face in a mirror ²⁴ and, after looking at himself, goes away and immediately forgets what he looks like. NIV

Chapter 2 contains a sudden 'ambush' of those who rely on deeds without faith-

- James 2:19 *You believe that there is one God.*
  Good! Even the demons believe that — and shudder. NIV

Chapter 3:1-12 contains an extremely sarcastic passage on the use of the *tongue-*

- James 3:2 *We all stumble in many ways.*
  Anyone who is never at fault in what they say is perfect,
  able to keep their whole body in check. NIV

This passage (3:1-12) ends with a set of six paradoxical parables-

- 7 *All kinds of **animals**, **birds**, **reptiles** and **sea creatures** are being tamed and have been tamed by mankind, ⁸ but no human being can tame the **tongue**.*
  It is a restless evil, full of deadly poison.

- 9 *With the tongue we **praise** our Lord and Father,*
  *and with it we **curse** human beings,*
  who have been made in God's likeness.

- 10 *Out of the same mouth come **praise** and **cursing**. My brothers and sisters, this should not be.*

- 11 *Can both **fresh water** and **salt water** flow from the same spring?*

- 12a *My brothers and sisters, can a **fig**-tree bear **olives**, or a **grapevine** bear **figs**?*

- 12b *Neither can a **salt** spring produce **fresh** water.* NIV

If James were a stand-up comedian reeling off jokes, his audience would be in stitches! But he isn't; he is using paradox, sarcasm and hyperbole to emphasise and re-emphasise the absolute necessity of taming the *tongue*. We must not be so taken up with James' humorous devices to forget about our own *tongues*!

Chapter 4 quotes a ubiquitous parable from Proverbs 3:34-

- James 4:6 … *'God opposes the proud*
  but shows favour to the humble.' NIV

God gives grace, or *shows favour,* to the *humble.* Who are they? Those who can laugh at themselves. If we want God to bless us, we must reject pride absolutely. If we want grace, we must be *humble.* If we desire divine *favour,* we must constantly check our motives for anything which may grieve the Holy Spirit (4:5).

Humour and humility are closely associated by James. Humility is, after all, the ability to laugh with God, at ourselves.

Chapter 4 ridicules the readers and tags another little parable on the end-

- James 4:14 *Why, you do not even know what will happen tomorrow.*
  What is your life?
  You are a mist that appears for a little while and then vanishes. NIV

One of the many uncomfortable things in James is how the richer Christians seem to have been treating their poorer brothers and sisters-

- James 5:4 *Look! The wages you failed to pay the workers who mowed your fields are crying out against you.* NIV

This personification of the unpaid *wages* is a 'shock tactic' to enable the bad Christian employers to recognise themselves, and repent. The personification is reminiscent of the Lord, Cain and the late Abel in the garden of Eden-

- Genesis 4:10 *The Lord said* [to Cain], *'What have you done? Listen!*
  Your brother's blood cries out to me from the ground.

10.3 I and II Peter

I Peter is about holiness in the face of suffering, and so is largely humour-free. But there is a little:-

- 1 Peter 4:3 *For you have spent enough time in the past doing what pagans choose to do — living in debauchery, lust, drunkenness, orgies, carousing and detestable idolatry.* NIV

The phrase '*enough*[262] *time*', or 'sufficient *time*', is a lovely piece of 'English' understatement, reminiscent of the comedian, Paul Daniels' riposte to a heckler-

> Heckler: *I don't like your suit!*

> Daniels: *Oh, I like yours; not a lot, but I like it!*

---

262 'ἀρκετὸς', enough, sufficient, adequate

Whenever it was that we bowed the knee to the Lord Jesus Christ, we need to make the best possible use of the remaining time. In one sense, everything before then was wasted.

****

2 Peter 2 alludes to Numbers 22 and *Balaam's donkey-*

- 2 Peter 2:15 *They have left the straight way and wandered off to follow the way of Balaam son of Bezer* [i.e. Beor], *who loved the wages of wickedness.* [16] *But he was rebuked for his wrongdoing by a donkey — an animal without speech — who spoke with a human voice and restrained the prophet's madness.*

God used a ridiculous talking *donkey* to rebuke, and make an ass of the *mad prophet*! Insult, irony and ridicule are all combined to warn Peter's readers about false teachers. Previously, Peter has likened them to brute beasts-

- 2 Peter 2:12 ... *They are like unreasoning animals, creatures of instinct, born only to be caught and destroyed, and like animals they too will perish.* NIV

Peter makes good use of the animal simile to teach that God is hunting them down. We once again the association of *donkeys* with fools in the Bible, as per King Saul[263], *Balaam*[264], and the Philistines[265].

For those who have, tragically, apostatised, Peter argues that their final state is worse than before they even claimed to be believers using a choice pair of proverbs[266]-

- 2 Peter 2:22 *Of them the proverbs are true:*
  'A dog returns to its vomit,' and,
  'A sow that is washed returns to her wallowing in the mud.' NIV

Presumably he uses sarcastic humour to denounce them because they are not simply victims, but vicious enemies of the genuine believers. It is surprising just how much scripture has to say on the subject of false teachers. We must make sure that we do not take the subject lightly.[267]

Some have taken Peter's brief mention of the apostle Paul to be funny-

---

263 1 Samuel 9
264 Numbers 22
265 Judges 15
266 From Proverbs 26:11 and somewhere extra-biblical.
267 See also Paul's swan song to the Ephesian elders in Acts 20.

- 2 Peter 3:16 … *His letters contain some things that are hard to understand, …* NIV

I think he is just being frank.

10.4 I, II and III John

As we noticed with John's gospel previously, John is loath to be humorous. Nevertheless, he seems to allow himself a little incredulity at *God's* amazing *love-*

- 1 John 3:1 *See what great love the Father has lavished on us, that we should be called children of God! And that is what we are!* NIV

At the end of his gospel, as we saw, John allows himself a little levity. Similarly, at the end of his third letter, he allows just the hint of a riddle-

- 3 John 13 *I have much to write to you,*
    but I do not want to do so with pen and ink. NIV

How can he write without *pen and ink*?-

- 3 John14 *I hope to see you soon, and we will talk face to face.* NIV

This is an important lesson for those of us who make far too much use of social media, email, telephones and texting. Face-to-face is usually better.

10.5 Jude

In verses 8 to 16, Jude seems to be using the same dismissive description of false teachers that we noted previously in II Peter. As Peter does, he points out that these are people who abuse humour by *scoffing* at everything that is good-

- Jude 18 … *'In the last times there will be scoffers who will follow their own ungodly desires.'* NIV

According to scripture, false teachers are to be recognised not just by their false teaching, because that is subtle and clever, but by their behaviour — *'ungodly desires'*. Part of such 'bad fruit'[268] is their use of humour, in this case *scoffing*.[269] What people laugh at can tell us a lot about their real attitudes.

10.6 Revelation

Surviving persecution is not a joking matter. John's apocalyptic vision contains very little that is humorous, but the letters to the seven churches sometimes make use of humour.

---

268 Isaiah 5:2; Matthew 7:17-18; 12:33; Luke 6:43
269 Also, grumbling and fault-finding (NIV) in verse 16.

A kind of riddle commending the *church* in *Smyrna*-

- Revelation 2:9 *I know your afflictions and your poverty — yet you are rich!* NIV

They have eternal life.

A warning to the *church* in *Pergamum* not to follow the mad prophet who was made an ass of by a donkey-

- Revelation 2:14 ... *some among you ... hold to the teaching of Balaam ...* NIV

An insulting rebuke to a *church* member in *Thyatira*-

- Revelation 2:20 *Nevertheless, I have this against you:*
  you tolerate that woman Jezebel[270], who calls herself a prophet. NIV

Another riddle, to the *church* in *Sardis* this time-

- Revelation 3:1 ... *you have a reputation of being alive, but you are dead.* NIV

The *church* in *Philadelphia* has no humour directed at it; they have little strength, but have remained faithful, so no humour is needed!

The *church* in *Laodicea* receives some well-earned vulgar humour-

- Revelation 3:16 *So, because you are lukewarm — neither hot nor cold —*

  I am about to spit you out of my mouth. NIV

Sometimes, we need some 'war-time' humour just to help us cope with all the difficulties of life. But, one day, all the miseries of life will be gone-

- Revelation 21:4 *He will wipe every tear from their eyes. There will be no more death or mourning or crying or pain, for the old order of things has passed away.* NIV

In the meantime, we must remain faithful and ready-

- Revelation 16:15 *'Look, I come like a thief!*
  Blessed is the one who stays awake and remains clothed,
  so as not to go naked and be shamefully exposed.' NIV

What kind of scary humour is that? It is slightly vulgar humour, laced with the shocking incongruity of being asleep and undressed when there is a battle happening! (16:14-16)

---

270 See 1Kings 21:23-25

There is triumphal laughter as the great enemy of God's people is defeated-

Revelation 18:2 … *"Fallen! Fallen is Babylon the Great!"* … NIV

Revelation 7 contains a riddle, but the riddle is not a question to be answered, in this case; it is the answer to the question, *"These in white robes — who are they, and where did they come from?"* (7:13) The curious answer is given by one of the 24 elders-

- Revelation 7:14 … *'These are the ones who have come out of the great tribulation; they have washed their robes and made them white in the blood of the Lamb.'* NIV

That riddle uncovers the heart of the gospel. These people have persevered through persecution, by trusting and obeying Jesus *the Lamb*. Their lives have been dyed a righteous *white*, paradoxically, through being *washed* in Jesus' crimson *blood*.

11. Conclusion

Humour is used fully and freely throughout most of the Bible. It is not used for light relief, but for the really serious moments and important truths. Only a small number of books are humour-free: Leviticus, perhaps Joel, the Song of Songs, maybe Ephesians and I Timothy, and II John. So, although it would be cavalier to say that the Bible is a humorous book, it is certainly true to say that it makes serious use of humour.

The narrative parts of the Bible contain the most humour, but so does much of Jesus' teaching. Perhaps it can be concluded that the Lord Jesus himself is the most prolific user of humour, followed by Luke and Moses?

If we fail to realise that some parts of the Bible are humorous, we stand to misinterpret them and misapply them. So to recognise humour where it genuinely occurs is essential, even crucial on occasion.

Here is a reminder of all the different categories of humour covered in this book:

Paradox, the Preposterous, Irony, Sarcasm, Hyperbole, Absurdity, Incongruity, Coincidence, Understatement (sometimes called Litotes or Meiosis), Insult, Taunt, Gloat, Surprise, Wit, Trickery, Juxtaposition, Ambiguity, a Joke, Slap-stick, a Pun, Word-play, a Riddle, Scorn, Shock, Teasing, Vulgarity, Recognition, Caricature, Spoof, Satire, Disbelief, Discomfort, Amazement, Incredulity, Triumph [271]

---

271 And this is hardly an exhaustive list, but it does appear to cover common kinds of humour in the Bible.

Beware! There may be more humorous categories than just these.

Each section you have read contains what preachers call 'application'. Consider reviewing these prayerfully. Scripture has very serious purposes.

Biblical humour is about laughing, with God, usually at ourselves. This is true humility and, as such, is the only way to be sure of God's blessing, grace and favour. When we give up the absurdity of trusting our ridiculous selves, and rely only on God, we can laugh with him at all his enemies, from the safety of his salvation. We can laugh at our sinful past; we can laugh at our triumphant future.

****

Also available on Amazon:

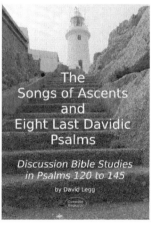

Printed in Poland
by Amazon Fulfillment
Poland Sp. z o.o., Wrocław